SURE AS
SUNRISE

SURE AS SUNRISE

Challenging thoughts for each day of the year

DERICK BINGHAM

Pickering & Inglis
LONDON · GLASGOW

Copyright © Derick Bingham 1980

ISBN O 7208 0468 X
Cat. No. 01/1834

First printing 1980

DEDICATED TO GORDON BRONTË

who,
though crippled with multiple sclerosis
still manages to give theology feet.

PREFACE

In March 1972 the persecuted writer Alexander Solzhenitsyn, then living in the Soviet Union, invited the Moscow correspondents of the *New York Times* and the *Washington Post* to interview him. This was a rare occurrence, indeed no journalist had observed him closely for five years. He was enduring the full wrath of the Soviet leadership, and, in his Moscow apartment, he talked about the fact that he and his family were 'a kind of contaminated zone' in the eyes of that leadership.

It was a most graphic and pained interview but one thing deeply impressed me when I read of it. Asked for his opinion of the young Russian writers Yevtusheuko, Voznesensky and Aksyonov who had aroused interest in the late 1950s, Solzhenitsyn pointed out that writers who deal with highly topical questions as opposed to 'themes of eternal significance' naturally fade from the limelight together with the issues they have treated.

So, I deliberately dip my pen into the 'themes of eternal significance', the things that outlast time and reach into eternity, not that I might be in any limelight but that he who is the author and finisher of our faith may be exalted. When everything else is obsolete and on the scrap-heap the love, grace, pity and power of the Lord Jesus will remain, exhaustless, indispensable and adaptable to the deepest needs of the human heart. I have found it so.

In this little volume I have ever sought to be practical with such 'themes of eternal significance' and may we together, by the grace of God, work them into the very bloodstream of our lives, one day at a time.

I wish to express my gratitude to Miss Carol Wright for typing this entire manuscript, and to Mima, Bob and Lorna who helped with the first draft.

Derick Bingham

The Secret Garden
  Alexandra Drive
    Liverpool

January 1

. . . And it came to pass
ACTS 9:32

I was driving through Portadown in Northern Ireland when I suddenly felt an urge to go and see a friend who was ill.

'Go and see Norman,' said a voice within me.

'But you may be in the way,' said another voice.

'I was sick and you visited me,' said a Scripture tucked away somewhere in the back of my mind.

I turned my car on the road and drove to his home. Norman greeted me weeping.

'I was just asking God to send you to me,' he said.

While Norman's good wife got the kettle boiling we overhauled the Universe together.

'Have you ever thought of the verse ". . . and it came to pass"?' asked Norman.

'It certainly occurs hundreds of times in the Bible,' I answered.

'Yes, but have you thought about it?' he asked insistently. Fame comes . . . to pass. Money comes . . . to pass. Suffering comes . . . to pass. Rain comes . . . to pass. Sunshine comes . . . to pass.'

He listed many things in life which come to pass. Then he paused for breath.

'What about the things which come to stay?' my friend then asked. Around that crackling Ulster fireside we quietly gathered our little 'bunch of everlastings'. Forgiveness of sins comes to stay. Salvation comes to stay. Jesus Christ himself is the *same* yesterday, today and forever. When he enters a life, he certainly comes to stay.

A few weeks later I preached Norman's text at his graveside. While I spoke on the theme '. . . and it came to pass' Norman was enjoying the indescribable presence of the one whose love will never end.

Friend, live this year for the things that come to *stay*.
HAPPY NEW YEAR!

1

January 2

Whatsoever he saith unto you, do it
JOHN 2:5

If Moses had been a committee, the children of Israel would still be on the other side of the Red Sea.

January 3

Thou wilt keep him in perfect peace, whose mind is stayed on thee: because he trusteth in thee
ISAIAH 26:3

My mother was dying. Cancer had brought her from a vivacious, outgoing, wholly dedicated and busy Christian life, to nights and days of unbelievable suffering. She cried herself to sleep for months on end.

Deeply disturbed I asked her what it meant to know and trust the Lord Jesus in such a situation. She smiled through her suffering and pointed to a text on the wall which bore today's text. 'That is what I feel,' she said, 'perfect peace.'

'There used to be a friend of mine,' mother continued, 'who was a missionary to China. She had a very thought-provoking translation for that text. It said "Thou wilt keep him in perfect peace whose mind stops at God".'

My mother died with such a faith and such a peace. Go out today, brother man, and live with it.

January 4

Be filled with the Spirit
EPHESIANS 5:18

Capernwray Hall, the famous Christian Conference Centre near England's beautiful Lake District is an amazing place. Recently I had the privilege of preaching there along with its dynamic founder and Director Major W. I. Thomas. He said something one evening which I have not forgotten. Talking about Calvary and the victory which our Lord Jesus Christ gained there, he said, 'The Lord Jesus did not die on Calvary just to enable you to get out of hell; he died to enable the Holy Spirit to get out of heaven into you.'

Be filled with the Spirit and only eternity will reveal what God will do in you and through you as this day passes.

January 5

Let your yea be yea; and your nay, nay
JAMES 5:12

Beware of the conversationalist who adds 'in other words', he is merely starting afresh.

R. Morely

January 6

Walk worthy of the vocation wherewith ye are called
EPHESIANS 4:1

I'd rather see a sermon than hear one any day,
I'd rather one would walk with me than only tell the way.
The eye's a better pupil more willing than the ear,
Fine counsel is confusing, but, example's always clear.

The best of all the preachers are the men who live their
    creeds.
To see good put in action is what everybody needs,
I soon can learn to do it if you let me see it done,
I can watch your hands in action, but your tongue too fast
    may run.

The lectures you deliver may be very wise and true,
But I'd rather get my lessons by observing what you do,
I may or may not understand the high advice you give,
But there's no misunderstanding how you act and how
    you live.

Anon.

3

January 7

I will not fail thee, nor forsake thee. Be strong and of a good courage
JOSHUA 1:5, 6

Are you facing a big decision in your life? Someone has described courage as 'a strong desire to live taking the form of a readiness to die'. In the Christian life the only way to save your life is to lose it in the service of Christ. No matter what it costs, seek first the kingdom of God and his righteousness in the decision you are about to make.

Acknowledge him, commit your way to him and then ask yourself two questions: Is what I am going to do *right*? Is it *necessary*? If the answer is 'Yes', go ahead, only 'be strong and of a good courage'.

January 8

As newborn babes, desire the sincere milk of the word, that ye may grow thereby.
1 PETER 2:2

Our twins when babies lived for their 'bottles'. Everything else was forgotten or set aside for the comfort of that bottle with its sustaining milk.

Do we desire God's word as a new born baby? Your condition as a Christian will be reflected by your desire, or lack of desire, for God's word. Toys amuse babies, but when they are hungry toys are useless. It is milk they want. If you are crying for spiritual food then television, novels, wordly-wise friends, or even 'meetingitis' will not feed you. You know where to go to get your food, Christian, so delay no longer. Desire and take the sincere milk of the word today.

January 9

Thou shalt not kill
EXODUS 20:13

It is the overtakers who keep the undertakers busy.

January 10

So teach us to number our days, that we may apply our hearts unto wisdom
PSALM 90:12

When as a child I laughed and wept,
Time crept,
When as a youth I grew more bold,
Time strolled,
When I became a full grown man,
Time ran,
As older still I daily grew,
Time flew,
Soon I shall find as I journey on,
Time gone.

January 11

And the ark rested . . . upon the mountains of Ararat
GENESIS 8:4

Noah's ark had no rudder. Right? Then it is quite clear that Noah had to go where God took him. Right? Where did God take him? To the mountain top. Right? If you go where God takes you you'll end on the mountain top as well!

(Alan Wilson, a physically handicapped boy [including handicapped speech] speaking at a special week for physically handicapped young people at Newcastle, Co. Down. July 1977.)   P.S. Right Alan!

January 12

Go ye into all the world, and preach the gospel to every creature
MARK 16:15

If you evangelise a man, you'll evangelise a person, but if you evangelise a woman, you'll evangelise a family.

January 13

But Joshua ... which standeth before thee ... encourage him

DEUTERONOMY 1:38

'Encourage him,' God said to Moses. It is a lost art, the art of encouragement. A simple word of encouragement can change a destiny. The famous Ulster cyclist Charlie Henderson says that his conversion to Jesus Christ at over 60 years of age was greatly due to a friend who encouraged him to put his trust in the Saviour as he was leaving a service after listening to a message from an evangelist.

Encourage someone today. If they have done something well, then tell them that they are doing a good job. If they deserve praise — give it to them. You may never get another opportunity. Everybody knows that it is not always *what* you say but the *way* you say it that counts. Do not be like the famous character Katherine Mansfield wrote about: 'He stands smiling encouragement, like a clumsy dentist.'

January 14

And the King was exceeding sorry; yet for his oath's sake, and for their sakes which sat with him, he would not reject her

MARK 6:26

It could be that today you are afraid to do what is right for the sake of those who are around you. You are 'exceeding sorry' like King Herod, but you would stop God's voice for the crowd's sake. Let Herod be an eternal warning. Because he was even more exceeding sorry as time hurried by. God never spoke to him again and the Roman Emperor later recalled him in disgrace, stripping him of his lands, palaces, position and influence. He lost everything.

'He is no fool who gives what he cannot keep to gain what he cannot lose,' said the missionary martyr of Ecuador, Jim Elliot. Herod was a fool. Don't you be one.

January 15

A certain Jew named Apollos . . . an eloquent man, and
mighty in the Scriptures . . . and . . . fervent in the Spirit
ACTS 18:24, 25

Apollos had three great qualities. I've met eloquent people
who were not mighty in the Scriptures. I've met people who
were mighty in the Scriptures but who were not eloquent.
Yet, I could count on one hand the number I have met who
were eloquent, mighty in the Scriptures and had that great
quality of early Christianity — fervency of Spirit. So the
message today is: you may not be eloquent or mighty in the
Scriptures, but you can be fervent for him!

January 16

Ye shall not surely die . . . in the day ye eat thereof . . . ye
shall be as gods, knowing good and evil
GENESIS 3:4, 5

When Satan tells a half truth, he wants us to believe the
wrong half.

January 17

. . . for, behold, he prayeth
ACTS 9:11

I've been to a good many Christian meetings in my time. In
great American cities, in dingy corrugated iron halls, in
beautiful homes and back street 'lean-tos', sitting in plush
cinema-type chairs and even on hard Korean floors. I've had
the privilege of hearing great preachers, marvellous
testimonies, beautiful singing and moving messages. Yet
never, anywhere, in any clime or nation, have I ever seen a
queue for a prayer meeting. Why?

January 18

I am ... the truth
JOHN 14:6

On many an occasion we probably all have stood near some harbour where people have been messing about in boats. No doubt you have seen the oil from the engines lying on the surface of the water. Oil will not be kept under, it must come up.

So with the truth. It cannot be suppressed. No amount of lying or cover-up can keep it beneath the surface. The truth will always come out on top. Preach the truth. Live the truth. Honour the truth. Do not ever be ashamed of the truth, for he, who will yet reign from shore to shore, is the truth.

January 19

The tongue is a little member, and boasteth great things. Behold, how great a matter a little fire kindleth
JAMES 3:5

Of all the problems in the Christian Church on earth, the havoc wrought by the tongue is the worst. 'They said' could be written over many a broken heart in every corner of the earth.

'The boneless tongue, so small and weak
Can crush and kill,' declared the Greek.
'The tongue destroys a greater horde',
The Turk asserts, 'than does the sword.'
The Persian proverb wisely saith
'A lengthy tongue — an early death'
Or sometimes takes this form instead
'Don't let your tongue cut off your head.'
'The tongue can speak a word whose speed',
Say the Chinese, 'outstrips the steed.'
While Arab sages this impart,
'The tongue's great storehouse is the heart.'

From Hebrew wit the maxim sprung
'Though feet would slip, ne'er let the tongue';
The sacred writer crowns the whole,
'Who keeps the tongue doth keep his soul.'

Anon.

January 20

*But thanks be to God, which giveth us the victory through
our Lord Jesus Christ*
1 CORINTHIANS 15:57

'What is our aim?' asked Churchill in his first speech as
Prime Minister in the House of Commons. 'I can answer in
one word: Victory. Victory at all costs, victory in spite of all
terror, victory however long and hard the road may be: for
without victory there is no survival.' And, indeed, victory
came.

    The lonely stranger of Galilee set his face steadfastly
to go to Jerusalem to die for your sins, to gain victory over
death, hell and the grave. His foe was greater than the
dictators and their war machines. His foe was the power and
person who inspires the dictators of this world and every
form of evil on the face of the earth. Our Lord Jesus
beheaded the giant, he defeated death and hell and he rose
from the grave the third day. What a victory! Enter into the
joy of it today, Christian, for because he lives all fear is gone.

January 21

Jesus saith unto her, Mary
JOHN 20:16

The Lord Jesus calls his own sheep by name. He did not call
Pilate by his name, nor Caiaphas, nor Herod, although they
were the 'big men' of the day. It is for his own that he
particularly reserves that honour. 'Mary,' he said. 'Master,'
she replied.

January 22

. . . *God is Love*
1 JOHN 4:8

In a Welsh valley, I sat beside him, along with a few other believers gathered together to remember the Lord Jesus in the breaking of bread. As worship continued I heard him sobbing. I'd never heard a man sob before, as he thought of Calvary. It was truly one of the holiest meetings I've ever known and even now memory recalls his huge frame bent over, his mind and heart overwhelmed with the thought of God in Christ loving him, even to the death of the cross. His name was Harry Bell. He was mighty in the Scriptures and knew them from cover to cover. When he left school his headmaster said, 'There goes a boy who could be a Prime Minister.' Yet Harry Bell gave his mind and strength to a higher order than earthly power. When it came to Bible exposition he had few equals in his generation.

One day he was lying in hospital and a friend came visiting. The friend, expecting some rare exposition, asked the great Bible teacher what truth he was enjoying that particular day.

'Oh,' replied the famous preacher, 'I'm enjoying a truth I learned in Sunday School.'

'What was that?' asked the visitor.

'Jesus loves me, this I know, for the Bible tells me so,' replied Harry Bell.

January 23

He that is not with me is against me; and he that gathereth not with me scattereth abroad
MATTHEW 12:30

'The Rt. Hon. gentleman has sat so long on the fence that the iron has entered into his soul.'
(David Lloyd George in the British House of Commons)

January 24

Give, and it shall be given unto you
LUKE 6:38

Give strength, give thought, give deeds, give pelf (money)
Give love, give tears, and give thyself.
Give, give, be always giving:
Who gives not, is not living.

Anon.

January 25

*Be not forgetful to entertain strangers: for thereby some
have entertained angels unawares*
HEBREWS 13:2

Do you not find that very often the people who are 'cracked
up' to be great turn out to be most disappointing when you
come face to face with them? It is true that the measure of a
great person is how they treat another person who can be of
no possible use to them. The great personalities of the
church of Jesus Christ sometimes fail miserably in this
particular area of behaviour.

   Of what use was Bartimaeus to Christ? Or Jairus'
daughter? Or Peter the fisherman? Or the woman with the
issue of blood? Or the thousands of ordinary folk who
surrounded him daily? In truth they were of infinite
importance and he took time with them. Let us follow his
steps. See how many strangers you can help today. You
might meet an angel or two before you get home.

January 26

Luke, the beloved physician
COLOSSIANS 4:14

When they forgot the Lord their God
1 SAMUEL 12:9

God and the doctor we like adore
But only when in danger and not before,
The danger is o'er, both alike rejected:
God is forgotten, and the doctor slighted.

Anon.

11

January 27

Let your speech be alway with grace
COLOSSIANS 4:6

Your talk travels on and on: and yet it goes no further than round the gooseberry bush.

January 28

And Saul was afraid of David, because the Lord was with him
1 SAMUEL 18:12

It is quite amazing how God reverses the ways of men when they trust him.

Saul had an army, he was King of Israel, he had a wicked temper and he twice tried to kill David by throwing a spear at him. David was young, inexperienced and heavily criticised by those nearest to him in his own family. The power and intrigues of the King and his Court were arrayed against him. One would have thought that David would have been afraid of Saul, but the text clearly states that it was Saul who was afraid of David. Why? Because the Lord was with David.

The lesson is clear. I'd rather have the whole world against me and God for me, than the whole world for me and God against me. The Lord *is* with you as you face the problems of today, so be sure your enemies are already frightened out of their wits.

January 29

Love your enemies
MATTHEW 5:44

When you throw mud at someone else, you are the one who is losing ground.

January 30

Let your light so shine before men, that they may see your good works, and glorify your Father which is in heaven
MATTHEW 5:16

Adlai Stevenson once said of Eleanor Roosevelt: 'She would rather light candles than curse the darkness, and her glow has warmed the world.'

Today, the darkness of some trial or tragedy may strike your life. When it comes don't curse the darkness but let the flame of his love, strength, compassion and grace shine out. Remember in the darkness what God has already taught you in the light.

January 31

The children of Israel sighed
EXODUS 2:23

Now Moses kept the flock of his father in law
EXODUS 3:1

What have these two verses in common? Harold St. John tells of hearing a Christian nurse from Japan relating an experience she had in a children's ward. She was trying to do the work of four nurses in an understaffed hospital, when passing down a ward, she heard a Japanese boy moaning: 'Nurse, it's very dark, very dark.' Her first impulse was to leave all to comfort him, but that was impossible. She whispered a few words to him about the Good Shepherd and hastened on. The Japanese boy sighed, while some Christian nurse kept the flock at home.

An hour later the boy cried again, 'Nurse, it's very, very dark.' Another word of comfort and the nurse hastened on. The Japanese boy cried, while some Christian nurse kept the flock at home.

The third time the nurse crossed over to the cot, and as the child went into eternity he muttered 'Dark, dark'. So the little Japanese boy died, and the Christian nurse kept the flock at home.

Are you that nurse?

13

February 1

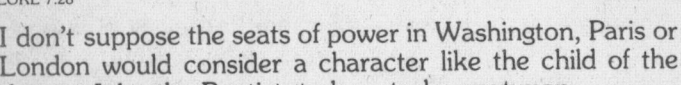

Among those that are born of women there is not a greater prophet than John the Baptist

LUKE 7:28

I don't suppose the seats of power in Washington, Paris or London would consider a character like the child of the desert, John the Baptist, to be a truly great man.

Yet God says he was 'great'. If this is the assessment of the Almighty what do you think was his reason for writing such a word over such a life? Have you ever seen a morning star? Watch it shine so solitary and clear in the sky. What do you think of when you see it? Surely the morning star tells you that a greater light is about to flood the earth. The sun will soon be up.

John the Baptist was great because every time people saw him they knew the Son of God was near. He pointed to Christ. Wherever you go today be like John.

February 2

Charity . . . and of faith unfeigned: From which some having swerved have turned aside unto vain jangling

1 TIMOTHY 1:5, 6

'Some having swerved,' says Paul. I wonder, could you and I be described as 'having swerved'?

Three boys once had a competition in the snow to see who could make the straightest snow tracks. Two sets of tracks swerved all over the place but one set of tracks was as straight as a good furrow.

'How did you do it?' asked the two whose tracks had swerved.

'Simple,' the third boy replied. 'I kept my eye on the farthest tree and as I walked towards the tree my feet followed my eyes in a straight line.'

If you and I keep our eyes on the Saviour we will not swerve aside from faith unfeigned to vain jangling. It's no exchange for a Christian, anyway. Is it?

February 3

Answer not a fool according to his folly, lest thou also be like unto him
PROVERBS 26:4

> The silly goat, so I have heard,
> Once kissed the fire, and lost his beard.

Anon.

February 4

Whatsoever a man soweth, that shall he also reap
GALATIANS 6:7

At a Bible Conference in Aberdeen John Lightbody, who shared in the ministry, told a story which sounded out with great warning to my heart. I can never forget it.

He said that in his village there was a family whose children were all dumb. When he asked his mother why such a thing should be she replied: 'John, when I was a child the father of the dumb children you speak of used to raid birds' nests, take the young and cut their tongues out. Now all *his* children are dumb.' 'Whatsoever a man soweth *that* shall he also reap.'

Be careful what you sow.

February 5

My grace is sufficient for thee
2 CORINTHIANS 12:9

> Sometimes the lions' mouths are shut;
> Sometimes God bids us fight or fly;
> Sometimes he feeds us by the brook;
> Sometimes the flowing stream runs dry.
>
> The danger that his love allows,
> Is safer than our fears may know:
> The peril that his care permits
> Is our defence where'er we go.

Annie Johnston Flint

February 6

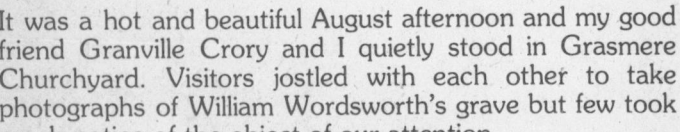

Behold the Lamb of God, which taketh away the sin of the world
JOHN 1:29

Him that cometh to me I will in no wise cast out
JOHN 6:37

It was a hot and beautiful August afternoon and my good friend Granville Crory and I quietly stood in Grasmere Churchyard. Visitors jostled with each other to take photographs of William Wordsworth's grave but few took much notice of the object of our attention.

It was a grave beside Wordsworth's that had brought us to that graveyard. On the headstone was a cross and wrapped around the cross was a lamb, while underneath, etched in the stone, were the powerfully moving words: 'Him that cometh to me I will in no wise cast out'. It was Dora Wordsworth's grave, the daughter of the great poet.

My heart moved within me as I read the words. There is a story behind them. Charlotte Elliot wrote the beautiful hymn 'Just as I am without one plea', and a friend sent the words to the dying Dora. Wordsworth could not bear to hear the words read aloud for he was not famed for being a lover of the Lord Jesus. Yet it is said that he had to admit that his daughter gained great comfort from the words, and died resting on the truth of the message they brought.

The great poet may be remembered for his poems and philosophy. Yet all his volumes of poetic fancy and thought have never brought the peace and joy which Dora and millions of people have gained from believing the truth of Charlotte Elliot's lines,

> Just as I am thou wilt receive,
> Wilt welcome, pardon, cleanse, relieve,
> Because thy promise, I believe,
> Oh! Lamb of God, I come.

February 7

All that will live godly in Christ Jesus shall suffer persecution
2 TIMOTHY 3:12

> You have no enemies, you say?
> Alas, my friend, the boast is poor
> He who has mingled in the fray
> Of duty, that the brave endure
> Must have made foes. If you have none
> Small is the work that you have done;
> You've hit no traitor on the hip;
> You've dashed no cup from perjured lip;
> You've never turned the wrong to right
> You've been a coward in the fight.

Charles Mackay

February 8

. . . He is able
2 TIMOTHY 1:12

Jeremiah thought he was too young. Moses thought he was too inadequate. Gideon thought he was too poor. Peter thought he was too sinful. Hannah thought she was too hard of spirit. Esther thought it was too dangerous. To all of them God proved that he was able, and the lives they led and the victories they gained in their day and generation proved that he was. He has not changed, even when confronted with the problems you have to face now. Believe me. He is able.

February 9

Come ye yourselves apart . . . and rest a while
MARK 6:31

'Slow me down, Lord' is a good prayer to pray. It is absolutely true that if you do not come apart and rest, you *will* come apart! Tired men are quarrelsome, so heed your Lord's command and rest awhile.

I have found that rest does not necessarily mean to stop working. Indeed, that is difficult to do if you find it hard to wind down quickly. No, a change is as good as a rest. 'Come apart,' said Jesus. Get out of the present environment and do your work in a different place. Change the furniture around, move your pictures, visit someone who would love to see you, but haven't for years. Ring someone and encourage them, write an inspiring letter. Shock the bus driver (or the chauffeur!), the dustman or the little lady behind the canteen by saying a cheerful 'Thank you'. Come apart and rest awhile.

P.S. Have a good day!

February 10

Who can find a virtuous woman? for her price is far above rubies
PROVERBS 31:10

> Tell me a thing she cannot dress,
> Soups, hashes, pickles, puddings, pies,
> Nought comes amiss, she is so wise.

Anon.

February 11

And God created whales . . . and God saw that it was good
GENESIS 1:21

Have you considered the majesty of this great creation? A baby blue whale at birth weighs five tons. One year or so later, after weaning, it weighs forty tons (which speaks well for the sustaining milk). If you drop the bones of a whale they will bounce because they are spongy and filled with oil. Sperm whales can go down half a mile and hold their breath for an hour and ten minutes. A whale's brain is a clever one but its size is smaller than yours or mine. Whales can rendezvous at an agreed spot in the ocean hundreds of miles from anywhere with an accuracy we would need radar to achieve. A whale lives about fifty years, reaching maturity at two years.

Why can a whale, which breathes air, die as quickly as a fish when stranded on a beach? Simply because while they are afloat they are buoyant and the water supports their weight evenly. On land whales' ribs crack under the strain. They die of internal injuries.

They are wonderful creatures and it is a dreadful pity men are slaughtering them by the thousands to get oil for margarine, and bringing the threat of extinction to these stupendous creatures of God's creation.

By the way, if the God who can create whales has promised to be with you every moment of the coming day, why on earth are you fretting? We, too, are fearfully and wonderfully made, and cared for.

February 12

The angel said unto him, 'Fear not, Zacharias: for thy prayer is heard
LUKE 1:13

I often think of poor Zacharias. He could not believe the news. He had prayed for a child and because the answer he wanted was so long in coming he thought God had forgotten. He very quickly learned that God does not forget our prayers, for his son John was born and mightily made ready a people prepared for the Lord.

How different was the reaction of Mary when the angel told her of the coming birth of the Messiah and Redeemer, our Lord Jesus Christ. 'Be it unto me according to thy word,' she quietly said on hearing the astounding news. Be like Mary and learn from Zacharias. When you pray, be careful what you ask for, because you might get it!

February 13

What communion hath light with darkness?
2 CORINTHIANS 6:14

It was in student days that I went to hear Dr Martyn Lloyd-Jones speak on the subject of unscriptural Ecumenism. I have heard heated words on the subject from many sources since. Yet, as long as I live I shall never forget the great expositor lift his finger and warn that uniting dead churches will bring nothing but death.

He reached the climax of his message and, stopping, he asked a question that has rung in my heart hundreds of times since: 'Tell me,' he said in his quiet Welsh accent, 'is Christ not enough for you anymore?'

> Saviour thou art enough,
> The mind and heart to fill.

February 14

The wicked have drawn out the sword, and have bent their bow . . .
PSALM 37:14

> I phoned a friend the other day,
> We talked 'news' you'd probably say,
> This, that and the other, we discussed,
> Nothing which would cause a fuss.

> Just 'mutual interest' was our agenda,
> Fresh events to each we'd render,
> Until I heard one which made me think,
> It dipped my pen deep into ink.

> 'My daughter's on a psychiatric ward,'
> 'On psychiatric,' the voice was lowered,
> 'There's a policeman's widow there at the moment
> They say her state is perpetual torment.

> 'Her husband was murdered before her eyes,
> The terrorists took him by surprise.
> Yet she *still* makes his lunch every single day,
> It makes no difference what others say.'

That policeman's murderer still carries on,
With his political war and party song,
How I wish I could bring him to the crunch,
And make him eat that policeman's lunch.

D.B.

February 15

*Ye also shall bear witness, because ye have been
with me . . .*
JOHN 15:27

At Queen's University in Belfast in the 1960s there was a
porter on the staff whom we will call Brian. He was a friendly
man and many a time we had a chat.

One day I ventured to witness to him about Christ.
'Don't talk to me about Christ,' he said. 'I'm not interested.
Fifty years ago I caught a Christian leader doing something
disgraceful and I've never had any interest in Christianity
since.' About three weeks later my friend Brian went into
eternity.

Bear witness today, Christian, but make doubly sure
that you do not bear *false* witness. There are eternal
consequences.

February 16

Casting all your care upon him; for he careth for you
1 PETER 5:7

God would constantly have us without anxious care. The
text always reminds me of the mother who worried about
her married son. 'But he is all right,' said her husband in
exasperation. 'He has a good wife to look after him.' 'Yes
dear,' she replied, 'but to tell you the truth I am not happy
unless I am worrying!'

Many people live like that. Worry is a sin and God has three answers to its curse. The first is faith. God is not ignorant of your need, and worry is a fruitless exercise. Have faith in God.

The second is 'casting'. You must take your hands off the problem, release your grip on it. Casting all your care upon him. Take your burdens to the Lord and leave them there.

The third is prayer and supplication, which is really the method of casting. Then the peace of God will do 'guard duty' over your heart and mind.

February 17

To be spiritually minded is life and peace
ROMANS 8:6

Always maintain the spiritual, in spite of the deadening influence of the transient.

February 18

This is the day which the Lord hath made, we will rejoice and be glad in it
PSALM 118:24

Life has many stages. The tender teens. The untiring twenties. The active thirties. The fiery forties. The forceful fifties. The serious sixties. The solemn seventies. The ageing eighties. The dying nineties. I do not know what stage you have reached but be sure of this — today is the first day of the rest of your life. Rejoice in it, and live it as if it were your last.

February 19

I bear in my body the marks of the Lord Jesus
GALATIANS 6:17

There are seven particular marks by which love to Christ is marked in a person's life.

1. They constantly *think* about him.
2. They love to *hear* about him.
3. They constantly *read* about him.
4. They delight to *please* him.
5. They are jealous for his name and *honour*.
6. They love to *talk* to him.
7. They long to be always *with* him.

The word of Christ comes to you today as it did to Peter that morning long ago at the seashore, 'Lovest thou me?' If you do, may you bear in your body the marks of the Lord Jesus.

February 20

Enoch walked with God
GENESIS 5:24

In my experience Japan is the most difficult country in the world for a Christian evangelist. In that country the indifference to the claims of Jesus Christ has to be seen to be believed. I stood one afternoon in a graveyard where 33,000 graves stretched out before my eyes and in a corner, in the 'Christian' section, there were only about three or four graves. It was frightening.

While travelling through Tokyo by train with my friend Tom Hill I asked him how he kept going in such a difficult situation. Tom had left great material prospects in Ireland after gaining an excellent University degree to go to Japan as a Christian missionary. What inspired him?

'I get depressed sometimes,' he said. 'I may not see great blessing or may never have the privilege of seeing many trust Christ but I do ask and long for one thing.'

'What is that?' I asked.

'That every day for the rest of my life I be allowed to walk with God,' he replied quietly.

I know of no greater ambition. Do you?

23

February 21

The proud he knoweth afar off
PSALM 138:6

That low man seeks a little thing to do,
Sees it — and does it.
That high man, with a great thing to pursue,
Dies ere he knows it.

                                        Anon.

February 22

Judge not according to the appearance
JOHN 7:24

A neighbour was passing my garden one day,
She stopped,
And I knew right away,
It was gossip not flowers
She had on her mind,
And this is what I heard her say.

'That girl down the street,
Should be run from our midst,
She drinks and she talks quite a lot,
She knows not to speak
To my child, nor to me,'
My neighbour smiled and I thought.

A tongue can accuse and carry bad news,
The seeds of distrust it can sow,
But unless you've made no mistakes in your life,
Be careful of stones that you throw.

Then a car speeded by and the screaming of brakes,
A sound that made my heart grow still,
For my neighbour's one child had been pulled from
    the path
And saved,
By a girl lying still.

The child was unhurt
And my neighbour cried out,
'Oh, who is that brave girl so sweet?'
I covered the crushed, broken body,
And said,
'The bad girl who lives down the street.'

Anon.

February 23

Honour all men
1 PETER 2:17

Great men never think they are great and
Small men never think they are small.

February 24

*In the morning sow thy seed, and in the evening withhold not
thine hand: for thou knowest not whether shall prosper,
either this or that, or whether they both shall be alike good*
ECCLESIASTES 11:6

A tinker out of Bedford,
A vagrant oft in quod,
A private under Fairfax,
A minister of God.

So wrote Kipling of John Bunyan. Strange how the influence
of this fifteenth century man is still around toward the end of
the twentieth century.

He had a seed to sow for God, and morning and
evening he kept at it, even when he was in prison twelve
years. It prospered in the hearts of millions around the
world.

25

B

One day Bunyan rode on horseback from Bedford to Reading to try to reconcile a father and son. He was successful, but on returning he was overtaken by a storm of rain and the chill he caught brought on a fever. Ten days later he was dead. Yet, the seed he sowed was never more alive. You have the same seed to sow today. Go to it!

February 25

The Lord blessed the latter end of Job more than his beginning
JOB 42:12

> I walked a mile with Pleasure,
> She chatted all the way,
> But left me none the wiser,
> For all she had to say.
>
> I walked a mile with Sorrow,
> And ne'er a word said she,
> But, oh, the things I learned from her,
> When Sorrow walked with me!

Anon.

February 26

Though he was rich, yet for your sakes he became poor, that ye through his poverty might be rich
2 CORINTHIANS 8:9

'With a suitcase full of clothes', wrote Hitler in *Mein Kampf*, 'and an indomitable will in my heart, I set out for Vienna . . . I too hoped to become "something".'

The world knows what that 'something' was. Yet without firing a shot or raising an army our Lord Jesus quietly entered the world, moved steadily to Calvary, and laid down his life for us. Through his poverty millions are now forever rich. How different he was! He did not come to 'be something' nor to be ministered unto, but to give his life a ransom for many. If it is 'something' you want to become, let it be something for him!

26

February 27

I commend unto you Phebe our sister . . . Priscilla and Aquila . . . Androcius . . . Julia . . . Apelles . . . Urbane . . . Herodion . . . Rufus . . . Patrobas . . . Hermes . . . Olympas . . .
ROMANS 16:1-15

In this amazing chapter there are names which I always have a horror of having to pronounce in public! Yet I must agree with William Brock when he said that this long list of 'Obscure' names proves something. They prove that Paul had one quality which great men do not always exhibit; he never forgot a kindness, and never forsook a friend. With Paul 'second fiddles' were priceless people. Are they with you?

February 28

Did not our heart burn within us, while he talked with us by the way?
LUKE 24:32

When some beloved voice, that was to you
Both sound and sweetness, faileth suddenly
And silence, against which you dare not cry
Aches around you like a strong disease and new
What hope, what help, what music will undo
That silence to your sense? Not friendship's sigh,
Not reason's subtle count . . . nay, none of these!
Speak, thou availing Christ! — and fill this pause.

Elizabeth Barrett Browning

February 29

David abode in the wood
1 SAMUEL 23:18

Near to my home there is a place called the 'Tipperary Woods'. It may not be the most famous place but when I go there to meditate I find it the most mind restoring place imaginable.

27

Can I ever relive my childhood's sense of wonder as with my friends we chased and played in this little plantation of Lord Annesley's? Roosting birds rustled over our heads. The Shimna river gurgled by. Then as dusk advanced, the light seemed to drain away like flood water. We stumbled home with weary legs across one of the many well beaten tracks in the wood. Home to warm pancakes and strawberry jam and bed. Thrushes said goodnight outside our window and dreams came of deep pools and woodland where it always seemed afternoon.

Recently I was in the 'speakers room' before going out to preach to the folk gathered at a Bible Convention in Belfast. Feeling nervous and viewing the prospect of the coming hour with trepidation, I was inwardly praying, 'Lord help me!' when, suddenly, a gentleman entered the room. He was a stranger to me but he approached with outstretched hand and a twinkle in his eye.

'Have you', he said, quietly, 'been down to the Tipperary Woods recently?'

That stranger will never know just what that question did to make me feel at home that evening.

March 1

Can there any good thing come out of Nazareth?
JOHN 1:46

Nathaniel had not yet learned that things are never really as they seem. Nazareth, the despised and neglected, did not seem like a place from which anything good could emerge. History proved different.

It is easy to accept things as they seem to be, but it is not right. Moses seemed to be a fool for forsaking the riches of Egypt for the wilderness, but he wasn't. David did not seem to be winning as he strode down the valley against the giant, but he was. Hannah seemed to be drunk in the eyes of Eli, but she was actually praying. The great enemy of the gospel, Saul of Tarsus, did not seem to be potential material for spiritual blessing but he became the world's greatest Christian.

Make a resolution that from today on you are never going to judge things as they *seem* anymore. I have a feeling Nathaniel learned his lesson.

March 2

And many of the children of Israel shall he turn to the Lord their God
LUKE 1:16

> My life shall touch a dozen lives,
> Before this day is done,
> Leave countless marks of good or ill,
> E'er sets the evening sun,
> This the wish I always wish,
> The prayer I always pray,
> Lord, make my life help other lives,
> Today.

Anon.

March 3

Launch out into the deep, and let down your nets for a draught
LUKE 5:4

'Are you coming fishing?' asked my friend Harold one morning. I am no fisherman but I went along to keep him company on the harbour pier at Newcastle, Co. Down.

I observed on arrival a long line of fishermen at the end of the pier. Indeed the intrepid Harold had to nudge his way in even to get a space to fish! I was sure lines were soon going to get crossed. It happened, and quite a few angry fishermen fumed as they struggled to undo tangled lines.

Harold fished on amid encircling feuds, determined to catch something. He did, it was so big that it took his hook, his line and his sinker. Indeed, recalling the incident now, I seem to remember it almost took Harold as well.

'Come back!' he yelled. I laughed until I was sore because, as you know, when a yacht is in full speed it doesn't exactly have brakes. Harold had hooked the sail of a passing yacht with one of his expert casts!

We had to retire from fishing that morning, but as I poked fun at my friend we reminded each other of Jesus' word to all of us who fish with the gospel for the souls of men in the world's great waters, 'Launch out into the deep'. A mile out in the sea you are not bothered with feuding fishermen and you do not get lines tangled. The truth is you are more likely to come home with a boatload of fish.

March 4

A father of the fatherless
PSALM 68:5

Many Christians who pray 'Our Father' on Sunday act like orphans the rest of the week.

Anon.

March 5

He hath sent me to bind up the brokenhearted
ISAIAH 61:1

Mending again!
Week in, week out, the pile is there
Of clothes that are unfit to wear
A button off, a rip or two,
And overalls with knees burst through.

Mending again!
Perhaps the same clothes fixed before
With buttons off and ripped some more
We sit and mend and soon we learn,
Like bread on waters, 'twill return.

Mending again!
Day in, day out, the Master mends
The Christian's life so full of rents,
Some caused by our own carelessness
A broken heart in deep distress.

Mending again!
How patiently he comes and mends,
With threads of love the selfsame rents,
Broken anew, bleeding and sore,
That he has fixed so oft before.

Clara Fennema

March 6

And Jesus ... took a child, and set him by him
LUKE 9:47

Shall I ever forget the night a young man came up to me after hearing a gospel message from God's word? 'Whatever shall I do?' he said. 'I am in an illegal organisation here in Northern Ireland and if I become a Christian what would happen to me?' I strongly advised him to trust Christ first and the illegal organisation would take care of itself.

That night he climbed the stairs to bed. Passing his son's bedroom he heard the little boy at prayer. 'Lord,' he was praying, 'save my daddy.' His little son's prayer touched his heart and quietly kneeling by his own bedside Christ as his Saviour. Today he valiantly serves the Lord as a missionary overseas, much loved, and much respected. A little child shall lead them.

March 7

A soft answer turneth away wrath
PROVERBS 15:1

Gentle words fall lightly, but they have great weight.

March 8

Set your affection on things above, not on things on the earth
COLOSSIANS 3:2

They allure me, the things of earth. They call me, the things of earth. They tempt me, the things of earth. But once one's soul has tasted of the things that are eternal; once one's heart has been captured by the love of the Lord Jesus, one is spoiled for the things of earth forever. Try them as I will, they never begin to compare with him. If I know it, then may I live it, and as you and I face the day, let us sing with Hartsough:

> 'I am resolved no longer to linger,
> Charmed by the world's delight;
> Things that are higher, things that are nobler,
> These have allured my sight.'

March 9

Now faith is . . . the evidence of things not seen
HEBREWS 11:1

I've heard many a description of faith but I like J. C. Ry.e's above most. 'Faith', he said, 'is the root and assurance is the flower.' Doubtless you can never have the flower without the root; but it is no less certain you may have the root and not the flower.

March 10

Be clothed with humility: for God resisteth the proud, and giveth grace to the humble
1 PETER 5:5

There is nothing as obnoxious as Christians who are proud. Let us be reminded that no beautiful garden or mansion is too beautiful or too well constructed not to be touched by decay. No person is too great to die and no character is too established not to be injured. Trust in the Lord with all thine heart and lean not to thine own understanding.

March 11

Bringing into captivity every thought to the obedience of Christ

2 CORINTHIANS 10:5

Guard well your thoughts; for thoughts are heard in heaven.

March 12

When thou sittest to eat with a ruler, consider diligently what is before thee: and put a knife to thy throat, if thou be a man given to appetite. Be not desirous of his dainties: for they are deceitful meat

PROVERBS 23:1-3

Maybe today, or this week, you will be called to dine with an ungodly man of influence and wealth. Do not let your guard down and be very careful not to overeat. The last few years in the history of our world should be ample warning that some rulers would stoop to anything to achieve their selfish aims; stoop even to using believers whose lives can be so easily trapped in their subtle schemes. Do not become a puppet of such either through their money, or the meat on their tables.

Be warned.

March 13

He which converteth the sinner from the error of his way shall save a soul from death, and shall hide a multitude of sins

JAMES 5:20

I wonder if you care for souls without Christ? Does it worry you at all? Have you ever shed a tear for a lost one? Many, many Christians seem to have lost interest in the lost. The following poem is a word to us all!

33

Could a mariner sit idle if he heard a drowning cry?
Could a doctor sit in comfort and just let his
    patients die?
Could a fireman sit idle, let men burn and give no
    hand?
Can you sit at ease in Zion with the world around
    you *damned*?

March 14

I am doing a great work, so that I cannot come down
NEHEMIAH 6:3

Day and night Nehemiah worked on the wall of Jerusalem. His army of helpers with sword and trowel greatly aided him, but the critics talked. Of course that's all they ever do. They wanted him to go to the valley of Ono for a discussion but Nehemiah firmly and wisely said 'Oh, no!' He trusted his Lord and pressed on.

    Are you being criticised, my friend? Are the critics sickening your happiness? Pay no attention for I'll tell you one thing, you never saw a statue put up to a critic.

March 15

The common people heard him gladly
MARK 12:37

It is a foolish thing to attempt to try to impress, and particularly to use the name of the Lord in your attempts. I well remember sitting in a tutorial with a Professor of Philosophy. He was particularly scathing in his remarks about Christianity and I thought I would try to impress him with a few facts concerning men of his intellectual ability who were outstanding believers.

    'What about Pascal, and his conversion?' I asked one day, knowing Pascal had been one of Europe's greatest philosophers.

'I am', he snapped, 'more interested in the conversion of the man in the street.'

I learned my lesson quickly. Little minds are interested in the extraordinary: great minds are interested in the commonplace. It was the common people who heard our Lord Jesus, gladly, and it seems to me things haven't changed.

Tell someone of him today.

March 16

Delight thyself also in the Lord; and he shall give thee the desires of thine heart
PSALM 37:4

As you look into your heart, what does it desire? Desires for your career, are they great? Desires for the welfare of your family are all, I'm sure, deep and honourable.

Perhaps some reader deeply desires marriage and is wondering about guidance. Perhaps you have a desire to enter upon some new project and wonder if it is right to do so.

Whatever your heart's desire, God says that first you must 'delight' yourself in the Lord. This means delighting yourself in his word, his work and his service. As you delight in him, very soon the desires of your heart will be for that which will bring him pleasure. It is true you will then get your heart's desire and no good thing will be withheld from you.

March 17

My soul, wait thou only upon God
PSALM 62:5

I remember the last time I ever saw David Craig, the famous Scot's evangelist. Drawing me near to his bedside he whispered, 'He whom thou lovest is sick.' It was true.

David Craig was always passing on helpful advice to young people and he gave me a piece of advice which I have never forgotten. 'When you go preaching', he said, 'always follow this rule. Wait in the presence of God until you get an impression, then when you get up in public God will give that impression expression.' It is advice which all of us could practise more, for we all preach some sort of message by the way we live and talk.

March 18

Be ye holy; for I am holy
1 PETER 1:16

Lord, make me as holy as a pardoned sinner can be made.'
Oft quoted prayer of Robert Murray M'Cheyne

March 19

Conformed to the image of his Son
ROMANS 8:29

Though sharp the blows, yet skilled the hand;
If we but feebly understand
The reason of each stroke,
How bless'd to know that he, who holds
The tools, before his eye beholds
His own beloved one!
The cares and troubles day by day,
The sorrows that o'ershade the way,
Together work for good.
For nothing e'er by chance befalls
The one whom God in purpose calls,
In whom his love is found.
But when we have the glory gain'd,
And Christ's full image have attain'd,
We'll praise his wondrous skill,
And bless the hand that dealt each blow
Upon the marble here below
In working out his will.

A.J.H. Brown

March 20

Let not your heart be troubled, neither let it be afraid
JOHN 14:27

The dignity of sorrow forbids the intrusion of any but the one who can truly sympathise, and his name is Jesus.

March 21

Whosoever therefore shall humble himself as this little child, the same is greatest in the kingdom of heaven
MATTHEW 18:4

As a little child relies
On a care beyond his own;
Knows he's neither great nor wise,
Fears to stir a step alone;
Let me thus with thee abide
As my Father, Guard and Guide.

Anon.

March 22

Caleb . . . wholly followed the Lord
JOSHUA 14:14

Can there be a greater compliment passed upon a life of a man than God's commendation of Caleb? When others scorned the idea of taking giants and walled cities, Caleb believed the promises of God. Others wholly followed themselves but Caleb wholly followed the Lord and did his will even to old age. 'Such', says the Bible, 'abide forever.'

Away with half-hearted Christian living! Let us, one and all, wholly follow the Lord this very day, no turning back.

March 23

Five barley loaves, and two small fishes: but what are they among so many?
JOHN 6:9

What are they? Only five barley loaves and two fish! Everyday, ordinary and commonplace things. Yet it is a good question. Just what are they? In the right hands they were enough to feed thousands of hungry stomachs. In the right hands they were enough to become the most remarkable five barley loaves and two fish the world has ever heard of! (I don't know of any I've heard mentioned more often! Do you?)

So it is in life. When the Saviour touches ordinary, seemingly insignificant lives — like yours and mine — he can use them to feed thousands of hungry hearts with spiritual food. He can make them into a force for good and turn the ordinary into something extraordinary. No life wholly committed to him is ever insignificant or ordinary.

March 24

The father of lights, with whom is no variableness, neither shadow of turning
JAMES 1:17

There is no shadow of turning with God. The Amplified Bible says, 'In the shining of whom there can be no rising or setting or shadow cast by his turning (as in an eclipse).' God is constant, 'I am the Lord, I change not' (Mal. 3:6). So, if God changes not, if his power and promises are the same and do not vary, if he is the unvarying light, why is there a distance between you? Who has moved away, God or you? Walk in the light as he is in the light and remember that the blood of Jesus Christ his Son cleanseth us from *all* sin.

March 25

And it came to pass after a while, that the brook dried up
1 KINGS 17:7

It seemed a catastrophe to Elijah, but then God does not always provide for his people in the same way and by the same means, lest they should rest in them and expect help from them. If God shuts one door, another opens; if one road runs out, why, just over there, look, is another! Elijah went to Zarephath and although for you it may be a new job, a new college, a new source of livelihood, be sure of this — the barrel of meal shall not waste, neither the cruise of oil fail, until the day that the Lord sendeth rain upon the earth.

March 26

Pure religion and undefiled before God is this, To visit the fatherless and widows in their affliction, and to keep himself unspotted from the world
JAMES 1:27

Religion. It is a word that evokes a thousand responses. Yet, the definition given is as far removed from the general attitudes to the meaning of the word as the North Pole is to the South Pole. Religion, God says, is visitation work amongst the fatherless and widows and keeping ourselves unspotted from the world. Tell me, are you religious?

March 27

Lord, is it I?
MATTHEW 26:22

There is sin in the camp. There is treason today!
Is it in me? Is it in me?
There is cause in our ranks to defeat and delay!
Is it, O Lord, in me?
Something of selfishness, garments or gold,
Something of hindrance in young or old,
Something why God doth his blessing withhold;
Is it, O Lord, in me?

March 28

Died Abner as a fool dieth?
2 SAMUEL 3:33

Poor Abner, he parleyed outside the place of security and blessing and perished. His mistake was not only that of parleying, but parleying with the enemy.

It should be an eternal warning to all of us that the enemy is not to be even nodded to. We must flee the very appearance of evil says the Scripture. Do not linger in the enemy's city like Lot. Do not even warm your hands at the enemy's fire, like Peter. Do not sleep in the enemy's lap, like Samson. Run, like Joseph, and for your soul's sake do not die as a fool, like Abner.

March 29

And when Abigail saw David, she hasted . . .
1 SAMUEL 25:23

Abigail heard of David's intention to sin in his anger. To her eternal credit she did not react as many believers do when they hear of a young believer who has committed some grave mistake.

Cries of 'I told you so' or 'He went up like a rocket, but we all knew he would come down like a stick', abound.

March 30

They all with one consent began to make excuse
LUKE 14:18

The first man mentioned in the parable of the great supper had to go and *see* a piece of ground. That was his excuse. With two good *eyes* he missed the blessing. The King allowed the *blind* to get it.

The second man had to go and prove oxen. That was his excuse. With two good *feet* he missed the blessing. The King allowed the *halt* to get it.

The third had married a wife. That was his excuse. With all the *attraction* of manhood that had gained him a wife, he missed the blessing. The King allowed the *maimed* to get it.

Be careful that you do not go through this day with an excuse for disobeying the Lord. He may give the blessing and reward for obedience which he had planned for you to someone with half the faculties and talent you possess. Remember the warning: 'None of those men that were bidden shall *taste* of my supper!'

March 31

He must increase but I must decrease
JOHN 3:30

'Until self-effacing men return again to spiritual leadership, we may expect a progressive deterioration in the quality of popular Christianity year after year till we reach a point where the grieved Holy Spirit withdraws — like the Shekinah from the temple,' said Dr Tozer. It is amazing how God drew Samuel aside and revealed the secrets of his heart to a child while Eli, the High Priest, slept. God still does such things.

Are you Eli, or that boy?

April 1

All things work together for good to them that love God
ROMANS 8:28

'Goo' day,' said 'e. 'Goo' day,' said I, 'an' 'ow d'you find
    things go,
An' what's the chance o' millions when you own a
    travellin' show?'
'I find', said 'e, 'things very much as 'ow I've always
    found,
For mostly they goes up and down, or else goes round
    and round.'

41

Said 'e, 'The job's the very spit o' what it always were;
It's bread and bacon mostly when the dog don't catch
  a 'are;
But lookin' at it broad, an' while it ain't no merchant
  king's,
What's lost upon the round-a-bouts we pull up on the
  swings.'
'E thumped upon the footboard, an' 'e lumbered on
  again,
To meet a gold-dust sunset, down the owl-light in the
  lane;
'For up and down an' round', says 'e, 'goes all
  appointed things,
An' losses on the round-a-bouts means profits on the
  swings!'

P. R. Chalmers

April 2

Give us this day our daily bread
MATTHEW 6:11

Daily bread is a gift but notice where it is placed in order of priority in the prayer pattern our Lord gave to his disciples. We ask that God's name be hallowed, his kingdom come, his will be done before we ask for daily bread. God's glory is preferred far above even our daily bread. No wonder it takes a born again person to pray in this manner. The natural man always seeks his own secular interest before God's glory. A worm cannot fly and sing as a lark: so a natural man cannot advance God's glory as a person elevated by grace does. The believer never prays this prayer as a chant.

April 3

I have loved thee with an everlasting love
JEREMIAH 31:3

Lois Walford Johnson, author of five Christian books, was told that she had cancer. The very mention of this disease brings an icy chill to one hearing about it.

I was moved to read what Lois said about how she reacted to the frightening news. She wrote that she entered hospital on a Sunday afternoon with this prayer in her heart:

> 'Lord, don't allow me at any time to feel separated from your presence. If I lose the awareness of your love, I have lost everything.'

April 4

Now there are diversities of gifts
1 CORINTHIANS 12:4

There was trouble in the workshop. The tools were having a row. Some blamed it on the hammer, he was much too noisy so he must go. But the hammer blamed it on the saw, he was constantly going back and forward. No, the saw would not be blamed, he accused the plane. The plane's work was much too shallow, always skimming the surface.

But the plane was sure there was someone else at fault, it was the screwdriver, because surely he was constantly going around in circles. The screwdriver said it was the ruler because he was always measuring other people by his own standard, but the ruler complained about the sandpaper whom he accused of rubbing people the wrong way. The sandpaper protested loudly and said that there could be no doubt that the drill was the culprit as everybody knew that he was so boring.

With that the carpenter arrived and the tools fell silent as he picked up each one in turn to finish the pulpit he was making. When completed it was mounted by many a servant of God who preached the word and multitudes were blessed.

April 5

Provoke not your children to wrath
EPHESIANS 6:4

A friend of mine was visiting All Souls in Langham Place, London, where a seminar was being held on marriage. A mother told how she had 'torn strips' off her daughter in front of some visitors, and, obviously, the girl had little chance of replying. In her heart the Christian mother knew she had done wrong. She knew that family discipline was not to be administered in front of the curious gaze of onlookers.

The next morning when she came down to breakfast she saw a note lying on the plate in front of her. It said more than all the books on child psychology have ever said:

> Dear Mother,
>   I hate you.
>   Love Lynda

April 6

Thy money perish with thee, because thou hast thought that the gift of God may be purchased with money. Thou hast neither part nor lot in this matter: for thy heart is not right in the sight of God
ACTS 8:20, 21

Simon the sorcerer was a big man around Samaria, but one day Philip the evangelist came to Samaria preaching Christ and Simon became a Christian and was baptised.

All was changed for Simon. The evil source of his former power was gone, the Lord Jesus was his Saviour. As he followed Philip around he was amazed to see the power of God at work in Philip's life. Peter and John came down to Samaria to help and the more Simon saw, the more he wanted to possess such power. Simon thought he could buy God's power and offered the apostles money for it. The ever-fiery Peter admonished him with 'the no holds barred' words of today's text.

To gain spiritual power one must lose. Abraham must offer up Isaac in order to hear the promise: 'In blessing will I bless thee.' Paul must suffer the loss of all things that he might 'win Christ'. Blessed are the poor in 'their self life' for theirs is the kingdom of heaven. Want to gain God's power today? Then lose your life for his sake and you will find it.

April 7

If the Son therefore shall make you free, you shall be free indeed
JOHN 8:36

There are four great freedoms which the Lord Jesus brings to all who trust in him.

There is freedom from fear. 'Fear not,' said the angel to Joseph. 'Fear not,' said the angel to Mary. 'Fear not,' said the angel to the shepherds who were 'sore afraid'. Live today with freedom from fear.

There is freedom of speech. The curtain in the temple was ripped apart when the Saviour gained the victory at Calvary. The way into the presence of God is now wide open for all who enter through the atonement wrought by the High Priest of our profession, the Saviour and friend of sinners. Tell him everything. No need of reticence when speaking to him face to face.

Freedom to worship is ours in Christ today. 'God seeketh those to worship in spirit and in truth,' said the Saviour to the woman at the well. She was a great sinner, had even argued with him about the Jewish-Samaritan question concerning the correct Holy Place to worship. Yet before she had talked with him very long she was worshipping him.

The fourth freedom is perhaps the greatest freedom of all — freedom from want. For the Christian who is enjoying this freedom his attitude is not to be forever listing the things he wants. Never! He cries, 'The Lord is my Shepherd, *I shall not want.*'

April 8

I have written briefly, exhorting, and testifying
1 PETER 5:12

We have, in this age of plastic and hurry, lost the art of letter writing. Have you considered, my friend, the power of a few lines written by a pen dipped in one's heart? Even God has communicated his truth to us through giving us his written word.

To you I say: write to some discouraged one, some broken-hearted one, some weary one, today. Exhort and testify like Peter did, briefly. But not only to the sad and lonely — the rich and successful too. You would be surprised to find how much they would appreciate it. So many are jealous of them that they never take time to treat them as people with real needs.

April 9

Jesus himself drew near, and went with them
LUKE 24:15

The hearts of those two on the way to Emmaus were sad. They were slow to believe, too. Yet Jesus came. It is so different when he comes. Never can his consolation be like the consolations offered to Tennyson in the awful hour when a close friend of his died. He was told, 'It might have been worse' 'these things cannot be helped'. Some even said, 'It is all for the best.' It did not help Tennyson's breaking heart. He wrote in despair:

> One writes that 'Other friends remain'
> That loss is common to the race;
> And common is the common place,
> And vacant chaff well meant for grain.
>
> That loss is common does not make
> My own less bitter, rather more;
> Too common! Never morning wore
> To evening but some heart did break.

That breaking heart may be yours. May the Saviour draw near and make it a burning heart before you switch out the light at the close of this day.

April 10

We know that we have passed from death unto life
1 JOHN 3:14

Why, muvver, why
Was those poor blackbirds all baked in a pie?
And why did the cow jump right over the moon?
And why did the dish run away with the spoon?
And why must we wait for our wings till we die?
Why, muvver, why?
Why?
Why?
This the high
Wail of the child with all his life to face
Man's last dumb question as he reaches space:
Why?

'We know,' says John, with Christian certainty. The Christian is no longer searching for the truth, because he has found it in Christ. 'Whys' for the Christian become 'wherefores'.

April 11

My God shall supply all your need
PHILIPPIANS 4:19

In my heart was a deep urge to write for children. Stories illustrating the gospel, attractively presented, was what I was after. To produce these I obtained the help of an illustrator and got to work on the writing. The printer got busy and the job was soon finished. His price was £250 and I told the Lord about it.

The phone rang one afternoon. Could I come and meet a friend in Belfast. I left home and drove to see my friend.

'Is there any work for the Lord in which you are involved at the moment which needs some money?' he asked. It was an embarrassing question for Christian work is not begging. 'Come on,' he coaxed, 'my wife and I were praying today and God told us to approach you with some money. We had it set aside for his work.'

'I am producing some booklets on the gospel for children,' I said sheepishly.

'How much?' he enquired.

'£250 actually,' I replied.

Drawing an envelope from his pocket and with tears in his eyes, he laid the little packet on the table.

'Inside you will find £250 exactly.'

April 12

Redeeming the time, because the days are evil
EPHESIANS 5:16

No time to read, no time to pray,
No time to serve the Lord today,
No time to teach in Sunday School,
No time — for life is very full.
No time to call upon a friend,
No time, e'en though he's near the end,
No time to share another care,
No time — for life is such a tare.
No time? How much is spent on self?
How much in gaining worldly wealth?
How much on seeking place and ease?
Say, friend, do you have time for these?

April 13

Where your treasure is, there will your heart be also
MATTHEW 6:21

'What were the happiest days of your life?' I once asked a wealthy businessman in a great city over the hills and far away.

'That's easy,' he replied. 'As a young Christian lad back in Ulster I used to go on a bicycle to give my testimony at meetings. If it was quite a distance I took the bus. They were undoubtedly my happiest days.' He said it all rather wistfully. It made me feel sad.

48

April 14

Charity . . . is kind
1 CORINTHIANS 13:4

> I would rather have one little rose
> From the garden of a friend
> Than to have the choicest flowers
> When my stay on earth must end.
> I would rather have a pleasant word
> In kindness said to me
> Than flattery when my heart is still
> And life has ceased to be.
> I would rather have a loving smile
> From friends I know are true
> Than tears shed 'round my casket'
> When the world I've bid adieu.
> Bring me all your flowers today
> Whither pink, or violet, or red,
> I'd rather have one blossom now
> Than a truck load when I'm dead.

Anon.

April 15

Thy will be done in earth, as it is in heaven
MATTHEW 6:10

How is God's will done in heaven? It is done by angels and they do it regularly, entirely, sincerely, fervently, swiftly, and with one single eye to his glory alone. If you want God's will done on earth as it is in heaven, do it angelically!!

April 16

Art thou he that should come? or look we for another?
LUKE 7:19

The question was honest. It was the imprisoned John the Baptist who asked it; the man who stirred the hearts of ten of thousands and drew them to the Lamb of God; the man who was the clear morning star on Israel's horizon heralding the coming Son.

'He shall be great in the sight of the Lord,' the angel

had predicted. Yet he made ready a people for the Lord and then wondered if he had pointed out the right Lord.

I doubt the man who has never wondered if all he believes in is true. The devil loves to taunt the Christian with doubt when he is weakest, particularly when depression or physical weakness comes.

When John's disciples delivered John's question to Jesus, he did not scold him for asking it. Rather he pointed out all the wonderful things his power was displaying. We never read that John doubted again. The proof for him and for us, is that this message works, this Saviour is alive. All that God pronounced he would be on earth — he was. His power is unlimited. In the light of this unalterable fact, the miserable beggar of doubt gets starved to death.

April 17

A man that hath friends must shew himself friendly
PROVERBS 18:24

> You may not sit in the halls of fame
> With honour to your name;
> You may not own a lot of wealth
> Nor even have the best of health,
> You may not reach some earthly throne,
> Nor claim a palace of your own,
> You may not master some great art,
> Nor rank with those the world calls smart,
> BUT YOU CAN BE FRIENDLY.

W.E.T.

April 18

I sat down and wept, and mourned ... and fasted, and prayed
NEHEMIAH 1:4

Nehemiah's soul was stirred! The gates of Jerusalem were burned with fire, the walls were broken down. The tears flowed down God's servant's face. He could not eat food. The condition of God's people broke his heart. What could he do?

He could pray. For four months he prayed day and

night to the Lord. As he carried wine to the King of Persia daily his heart longed, not for the extension of the Persian Empire, but for the extension of the kingdom of God.

Then God acted, for remember the initiative is always with God, not with us. Instead of Nehemiah mentioning the problem of getting away from the Persian Court to do God's will and work, the king mentioned it to him and the door of opportunity opened wide.

So let this be our attitude today. Leave the initiative for opening doors with God and as sure as you are reading these lines God will use you mightily yet. Ours is to get on with the legitimate duties of the day. No matter what they are, do them as unto the Lord, carefully, enthusiastically and prayerfully.

April 19

Not I, but Christ
GALATIANS 2:20

I often think of Augustine. Though followed by a mother's prayers, he had wasted many an hour in immorality. But those prayers found their mark, as all mothers' prayers do, and eventually Augustine was born again.

Passing through one of his old haunts, a girl came running to him shouting: 'Augustine! Augustine! It is I, it is I.'

Quietly Augustine turned to her and said: 'It is not I . . . but Christ that liveth in me.'

Such are the words of a life hidden with Christ in God.

April 20

Let thy words be few
ECCLESIASTES 5:2

A friend of mine, Kenneth Johnston of Stramore, Guilford in Northern Ireland, once told me of an old man in the west of Ireland from whom he buys sheep. One day the man asked what one should take as a guide concerning general conversation.

'Only say what is necessary,' Kenneth replied.
It is as good a guide as I know.

April 21

The contention was so sharp between them, that they departed asunder one from the other
ACTS 15:39

> To dwell above with the saints we love,
> That certainly will be glory,
> But to dwell below with the saints we know,
> That's quite another story.

April 22

No man can serve two masters
MATTHEW 6:24

We sat around the table, talking. In the afternoon we had been busy telling of the Saviour's love and my host was rejoicing in the crowd that had turned out, and the seeming success of a happy afternoon spent in the Lord's service.

'I used to be up to the neck in politics,' he said. 'Morning, noon and night my energies were spent in pushing my political views. Then my wife took ill and almost died. I tell you, brother, politics lost its grip immediately. I've never been the same since. We're busier in the Lord's service than ever before.' The huge beam on his face proved it.

Consider, Christian, are you, too, entangled with the affairs of this life? A good long look at death and the hereafter would soon change your tune towards eternal values.

April 23

Took his journey into a far country, and there wasted his substance . . .
LUKE 15:13

If you do not find pixies on your own doorstep: you'll never find fairyland.

F. W. Boreham

April 24

Thy servant slew both the lion and the bear
1 SAMUEL 17:36

David's greatest success story must have been the day he slew Goliath. For centuries men, women and children have thrilled to the story of the sling, the stone and the lad who slew the giant.

I would not in any way detract from the victory of that wonderful day, but always remember that before God would use you in public to slay giants, you have to slay lions and bears in private.

April 25

Let us rise up and build
NEHEMIAH 2:18

Who comprised the 'us' in this verse? Read the names in chapter 3. I had publicly to expound this chapter once and to be honest with you I was going to skip it. Long, difficult-to-pronounce names will interest no one, I thought.

Then I was led to observe that 'Halohesh, the ruler of the half part of Jerusalem, and his daughters' were working on the wall. Women were busy in God's work. I noticed also that Meremoth repaired one part of the wall (3:4) and then another (3:21). The Tekoites did the same. No laziness in God's work.

Then what about the 'sixth son of Zalaph'? Where were the other five brothers who are not mentioned? I don't know, but in God's book those are most honourable who are most useful in God's work.

'After him Baruch ... earnestly repaired the other piece.' Earnestness in God's work!

What about Meshullam who repaired ... over against his chamber? (3:30). This man had only a bedsitter in Jerusalem, but he repaired it. He knew the slightest gap in the wall and the enemy would come in like a flood. Vigilance in small duties in God's work!

So it was that the long list of names in chapter 3 became a treasure house of inspiration to work for God.

April 26

We shall not all sleep, but we shall all be changed
1 CORINTHIANS 15:51

For five days we had been together studying the word of God, 25,000 of us. God's servant had closed his final message.

I was sitting in my seat, pretty exhausted with the intensive teaching, when it was announced that we were all to be given a present. It was a little badge (trust the Americans) with the letters PBPGINFWMY boldly inscribed on it. What did it mean?

'Please be patient God is not finished with me yet'

I wear it sometimes, especially when my critics are around!

April 27

Wine is a mocker, strong drink is raging: and whosoever is deceived thereby is not wise
PROVERBS 20:1

In the United Kingdom alone in the last eight years wine consumption has gone up by 152%, spirit consumption by 68%, beer drinking by 33%. In the year I am writing £2000 million has been spent on alcohol, and £20 million advertising it. There are 4000 known alcoholics and there have been 80,000 arrests for public drunkenness and 30,000 arrests for drunken driving. Despite warnings of cirrhosis of the liver, pneumonia, heart disease through alcohol, millions go on unheeding.

Heaven help you, Christian, if you are guilty by 'social drinking' of introducing your children or friends to the mocking raging curse.

April 28

To every man according to his several ability
MATTHEW 25:15

An airline pilot does not make the coffee for the passengers. He gets on with the flying. A school teacher does not build extensions to his classroom. He leaves that to the builder. A ship's captain does not usually need to haul at a rope, it is enough for him to steer.

Use your own gift and do not envy others theirs.

April 29

Where art thou?
GENESIS 3:9

Hugh Lindsay of Carryduff in Northern Ireland, is, as we say in our country, 'a rare man'. He detests the front row in anything and loves to work for God behind the scenes.

The other day he drove his car up to my front gate and tooted the horn. When Hugh toots you have to uproot! I ran down to the gate and got into his car.

'I want to tell you a story,' he said. 'A German Bible teacher was lecturing a lot of young preachers about the importance of the right attitude of heart when preaching.

'Gentlemen, please rise one after the other and let me hear how you would say "Adam where art thou?" if preaching on that text,' he asked.

One after another they rose and did their bit.

'Gentlemen,' said the Bible teacher, 'sit down. You have all said it in the wrong way, because *God is not a policeman!*

'There are too many preachers in this land who make people think God is a policeman,' Hugh said, quietly, and with that we parted.

It was a lesson I shall not forget.

April 30

Love your enemies
MATTHEW 5:44

If you want to hit a person a knock-out blow today because you detest him, hit him with an act of loving kindness.

May 1

Because iniquity shall abound, the love of many shall wax cold
MATTHEW 24:12

Is there anything worse than love grown cold?

Here is a woman who used to rush to say goodbye to her husband at the gate in the mornings. Now she merely nods from an upstairs window.

There, perhaps, is the husband who used to bring home the surprise gift or pass the kindly word of appreciation, but those days are long since gone.

Here is a teenager who once appreciated the warm security of home but now he is trying the things which his parents were attempting to save him from, and his love for his parents has grown cold in the process.

The Lord Jesus warned that as time would continue iniquity would increase. So today iniquity is abounding and many Christians are beginning to give in to the surrounding climate. They have grown cold in their love for God.

If we know the tragedy of human love growing cold how much worse is the coldness of a waning love for God? Wherever you find yourself, do not ever let the profanity in your office, the 'muck-raking' of the secular press, the poison of gossip or even the aloofness of casual Christians move you to coldness of love toward God.

May 2

Let each esteem other better than themselves
PHILIPPIANS 2:3

William Gilmore, evangelist and Bible teacher, was fond of children. I well remember his kindness to me as a child and that unforgettable day when he presented me with my first penknife. By such acts are great men remembered when their sermons are long forgotten!

When I think of how men forget the truth of today's text, it reminds me of a remark William Gilmore once made.

'What would you like for tea, Mr. Gilmore?' asked a lady.

'What all the brethren like,' he replied.

'And what on earth do all the brethren like?' she asked, anxiously.

'A little bit of plaice!' grinned the preacher.

May 3

The valley of the shadow of death
PSALM 23:4

Is death near? Has this little volume slipped into hands who prop it up on a bed where death is lurking? The fact is, if it were only realised, death is near to us all. Eternity is but a heartbeat away. If you are resting in Christ, fear not. A shadow cannot bite. A shadow cannot destroy. It is only the valley of the shadow, David tells us.

To have a shadow you must have a light. So, there must be a light shining in this valley and there is no question about it, this light is from the glory dwelling in Immanuel's land. You are on the edge of the greatest experience you have ever known. Rest, today, in this thrilling assurance.

May 4

Onesiphorus ... was not ashamed of my chain
2 TIMOTHY 1:16

Some Christians know nothing about being identified with the sufferings of Christ. For them Christianity is regular attendance at their place of worship and very little else.

Paul speaks often of those believers who were ashamed of his prison record. They wanted the blessings of the gospel but not the sufferings or the persecutions and ridicule that arises when Satan's territory is truly invaded.

On this occasion of Paul's very last letter on earth he commends Onesiphorus. When every Christian was fleeing from Nero's Rome, Onesiphorus was diligently searching every prison in Rome for the persecuted Paul. 'He sought me out diligently and found me,' writes Paul, forever immortalising the humble Onesiphorus for his brave action.

Find some persecuted one today, Christian. Search for him diligently until you find him and never, ever in your life, be ashamed of such.

May 5

Be careful for nothing; but in every thing by prayer and supplication with thanksgiving let your requests be made known unto God
PHILIPPIANS 4:6

Amy Carmichael was lying awake one night worrying about something. The clock seemed to say as it ticked:

Commit your care, commit your care,
For I am here, and I am there.
Commit, commit, and do not fear,
For they are dear and you are dear.

The next night, she says, the clock seemed to say different words,

Where is your care? Where is your care?
You cannot find it anywhere,
You cannot find it anywhere,
I heard your prayer, I heard your prayer.

May 6

He that soweth to his flesh shall of his flesh reap corruption; but he that soweth to the Spirit shall of the Spirit reap life everlasting
GALATIANS 6:8

Our English teacher at school used to tell us that whatever we went in for we would get. He was, of course, absolutely right. Meditate on today's verse and think of the implications.

Two natures struggle in my breast
The one is foul, the other blest;
The 'new' I love, the 'old' I hate;
The one I feed will dominate.

May 7

Peter went out, and wept bitterly
LUKE 22:62

After speaking from God's Word to a group of children, a child approached me, anxiously, with a question:

'Mister, how many chances does God give you to be good?'

A profound question. Peter sinned three times by carnal fear, but repented and had forgiveness of the Lord. Within weeks of his great denial he stood in Jerusalem and witnessed a great confession to the eternal blessing of multitudes.

If you have time today, steal away somewhere and quietly read Nehemiah chapter 9. Notice how many times God forgave his stiffnecked stubborn people when they repented. Despite their failure he blessed them, time and again.

He will definitely do it for you also. But, remember, although God forgives when we sow wild oats, he doesn't cancel the harvest of sorrow.

May 8

Lay up for yourselves treasures in heaven . . .
MATTHEW 6:20

In the spiritual, as in the secular, you quickly lose interest if you have nothing invested.

May 9

Though your sins be as scarlet, they shall be as white as snow
ISAIAH 1:18

Harry Andrews is a Christian of rare gifts. No preacher I have ever known can tell a story like Harry tells it. Recently I rang him on the telephone to see if he could tell me a story illustrating our text.

'Many years ago', said Harry, 'British soldiers were marching from Clifton Steet to the docks in Belfast. A gentleman was chatting to the owner of a chemist's shop as the soldiers passed by.

'What lovely white tunics those soldiers are wearing,' said the gentleman.

'White tunics!' exclaimed the chemist. 'They are not white tunics, they are scarlet!'

'I must be seeing things,' said the gentleman.

'No, you're not,' replied the chemist, smiling, 'you are just looking at scarlet through the scarlet pane of glass in my window. When you look at scarlet, through scarlet, it turns white!'

So God looks at one who has received the Saviour through the work of Calvary and things are different. Scarlet, through scarlet, turns white. In fact as white as snow.

60

May 10

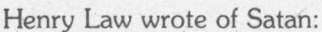

Henry Law wrote of Satan:

> He never slumbers, is never weary, never relents, never abandons hope. He deals blows alike at childhood's weakness, youth's inexperience, manhood's strength and the totterings of age. He watches to ensnare the morning thought. He departs not with the shades of night.
>
> By his legions he is everywhere at all times. He enters the palace, the hut, the fortress, the camp, the fleet. He visits every room of every dwelling, every pew of every sanctuary. He is busy with the busy. He hurries about with the active. He sits by each bed of sickness, and whispers in each dying ear. As the spirit quits the tenement of clay, he still draws his bow with unrelenting rage.

What I say unto you, I say unto you all — *watch*.

May 11

Again and again people are faced with temptations and they feel that those temptations are peculiar to them alone. 'Nobody else could ever think such things as I think' is the common cry. 'No one could ever know the rotten feelings I have when I see how I respond to temptation' is a common comment.

Banish such thinking. Temptation is common to man, in every form. There is nothing new under the sun. Just remember that God does not tempt you. You are tempted when you are drawn away of your own desire and enticed. God will not tempt you but he will always provide a way of escape out of every temptation.

61

May 12

Rejoice with them that do rejoice, and weep with them that weep
ROMANS 12:15

The day dawned bright and clear and a friend came bouncing into my home rejoicing in a beautiful new property which he had bought.

'Let's go and walk around it,' he said. I went with him and can honestly say that I rejoiced with him as we walked in its spacious grounds, stood by the river which runs through the grounds and inspected the host of daffodils which were eager to start showing their presence as a first sign of spring.

Two hours later I stood by a family who grieved deeply at the death of a loved one. I felt tears creep into my eyes as I saw the sting of death.

Every day you live you will come across both kinds of experiences in your circle of friends and acquaintances. Life is made up of breathtaking joys and heartbreaking sorrows. Be ready, by the grace of God, for both.

May 13

Let not your heart be troubled: ye believe in God, believe also in me. In my Father's house are many mansions: if it were not so, I would have told you. I go to prepare a place for you.
JOHN 14:1,2

Living amidst the troubles of this province of Northern Ireland I think I know a little of the frustrations our young people face. I know that Catholic and Protestant live like black and white. I know what it is to talk to a prisoner in an internment camp one day, and shake hands with a young widow who has just lost her husband in a booby trap explosion the next. I know what it is to have to sit in a mental institution with a student teacher whose nerves have been wrecked by living in a troubled city. I know I'm sick to death of it too.

Can you blame me then if my heart beats a little faster when I read the words of our text. They are the words of the

Lord Jesus about heaven, and I believe him. If the tragedies of this Ireland in which I live, the sin that surrounds me, were to have an end in the grave with no life beyond the grave, I would consider living pointless. The Son of God taught that there is a life beyond death. There is a place, actual and literal, where there is no sin, no sorrow, no night, no tears, no terror, no death.

May 14

And, having made peace through the blood of his Cross
COLOSSIANS 1:20

The noise was different from any that ever had fallen on my Irish ears before. It was weird, high pitched, monotonous and repetitive. I was irresistibly drawn. It was Eastern music.

Walking slowly up the narrow street I turned a corner to see what amounted to about two thousand Chinese eyes watching a stage. It was part of a heathen festival and gaudily dressed men were dancing up and down with exuberance and shouting their monotonous song. I sat down to watch, fascinated.

A Chinese wandered over and asked if I wanted a beer. I smiled and shook my head but added that I was extremely partial to Coca Cola. It soon appeared and a boy with it. He spoke fluent English and asked me if I was interested in their religion. I replied that I was very curious about what was going on.

He took me into their temple. The smell of incense was heavy and sickening and the area in front of the place where he told me the gods were was just heaped with gifts. These were given by the people to the gods and then auctioned off at twice the price to those who had given them. This, my new friend told me, pleased the gods.

He then handed me a piece of paper on which I could see the mark of human blood. This had come from the cut wrists of men in a spiritual trance. If I put that on my door I would have peace, I was told. Tears came to my eyes, and looking at him I explained quietly and gently that Jesus Christ had shed his blood for me and through the shedding of his blood I had peace, and not only peace in my heart but peace with God. Never as long as I have breath, will I forget his answer.

'You are lucky,' he said. 'Your religion is so uncomplicated. I have to worry about my ancestors. Your religion is so easy.'

I thought of my home where my mother taught me the Scriptures and how I could be saved by believing on the Lord Jesus Christ. This Chinese lad thought it too simple; yet for the door to be opened it was no easy matter for the Saviour. It cost him everything.

May 15

Mary hath chosen that good part, which shall not be taken away from her
LUKE 10:42

My mother was not a philosopher or a great theologian in terms of the great women in the history of the Church, but as far as I, and those who were privileged to be near her were concerned, the spiritual things she taught us will be forever in our hearts.

One day she came running into my room, Bible in hand.

'Look at this,' she exclaimed.

'Look at what?'

'The story of Mary and Martha.'

For twenty minutes she sat down and poured out some gleanings she had gained from her quiet reading of the story. My mum had little time for commentaries and read little but pure Scripture. The point she emphasised to me that day was what Jesus said of Mary, who sat at his feet. He said that she had chosen that better part, which shall not be taken away from her! Looking at me with determination mother declared:

'Shall not be taken away in time or eternity! To sit at Jesus' feet is an eternal blessing! What you gain there you simply cannot lose. It goes on with you forever. It will *never* be taken away from you, son!'

May 16

I resolve by the grace of God:
1. Never to judge others 1 Corinthians 4:3-5
2. Never to discuss the faults and failings of absent ones Proverbs 16:28
3. Never to divulge secrets Proverbs 11:13
4. Never to repeat a matter Proverbs 17:9
5. Rather to remain silent when there is nothing that I can say to another's advantage Titus 3:2
6. To set a watch upon my lips Psalm 39:1
7. Always to attribute the best motives 1 Corinthians 13:7
8. To talk less and listen more
9. To take time to be friendly
10. To be uniformly courteous
11. To shun debt
12. To do an hour's solid reading
13. To cultivate patience
14. That should I fail in any one of the above resolutions, to repent and confess it immediately, and if necessary, to ask an injured brother's forgiveness.

May 17

No man, having put his hand to the plough, and looking back, is fit for the kingdom.
LUKE 9:62

There may be someone reading this book who is ready to give in to something they know to be wrong. Let me tell you a story from the life of Catherine Booth. She was present at a large conference of the Salvation Army. A compromise was suggested, which, in effect, meant her husband giving up full-time evangelism. She would not be party to the compromise. Rising from her seat in the gallery, Mrs Booth's clear voice rang out as she said to her husband, 'Never!'.

There was a pause of bewilderment and dismay. Every eye was turned toward the speaker in the gallery. The idea of a woman daring to utter a protest produced something little

65

short of consternation. It was a sublime scene as with flushed face and flashing eye she stood before that audience. Decision, irrevocable and eternal, was written upon every part of that powerful and animated countenance. Her 'Never!' seemed to penetrate like an electric flash through every heart.

My message to you today, Christian, is never give in! Never — in anything great or small, large or petty — never give in except to convictions, honour, good sense and the will of God.

May 18

Now is the accepted time
2 CORINTHIANS 6:2

A botanist sallied forth to the hills to study his favourite flowers. Presently he plucked a heather bell and put it upon the glass of his microscope. He stretched himself at full length upon the ground and began to scrutinize it carefully. Moment after moment passed, and still he lay there gazing, entranced by the beauty of the little flower.

Suddenly a shadow fell upon the ground where he lay. Looking up, he saw a tall, weather-beaten shepherd gazing down with a smile of half-concealed amusement at a man spending his time looking through a glass at so common a thing as a heather bell.

Without a word the botanist reached up and handed the shepherd the microscope. He placed it to his eye and began to gaze. For him, too, moment after moment sped by while he gazed in enraptured silence. When he handed back the glass the botanist noticed that the tears were streaming down the shepherd's bronze cheeks.

'What's the matter?' asked the botanist. 'Isn't it beautiful?'

'Beautiful,' said the shepherd. 'It is beautiful beyond all words. But I am thinking of how many thousands I have trodden under foot!'

Priceless opportunities come. We trample upon them, and they are lost forever!

66

May 19

He shall direct thy paths
PROVERBS 3:6

Peter Marshall came from a town called Coatbridge in Scotland. One misty evening he was returning home from night school and his pathway took him across some fields. The mist was very thick and before long he was quite lost. Suddenly through the misty air he heard a voice distinctly call: 'Peter!' He stopped and looked around. All he could see was mist and certainly nobody was there. He went to move on when it came again, clear, distinct and definite: 'Peter!' He put out his foot and suddenly there was no more ground. He drew back and falling to his knees began to crawl forward. In a few seconds he realised he was on the edge of a sheer cliff. The voice had saved his life. In later life Peter Marshall, chaplain to the U.S. senate, believed that voice was the voice of God.

May 20

A man's gift maketh room for him
PROVERBS 18:16

If you can't be a pine on the top of the hill,
Be a scrub in the valley — but be
The best little scrub by the side of the rill:
Be a bush if you can't be a tree.

If you can't be a bush, be a bit of the grass,
Doing something for somebody's sake.
If you can't be a muskie, then just be a bass —
But the liveliest bass in the lake!

We can't all be captains, some have to be crew,
There's something for all of us here,
There's big work and little for people to do,
And the task we must do is the near.

If you can't be the highway, then just be a trail,
If you can't be the sun, be a star:
It isn't by size that you win or you fail —
Be the best of whatever you are!

Anon.

May 21

Two are better than one
ECCLESIASTES 4:9

We often tend to act first and ask questions later. Yet this is something that tends to smash, to destroy, to annihilate, all that a man has seen, known, loved, enjoyed or hated; something which could sweep the whole precious world utterly away from his sight by a simple and appalling act.

Irrevocable decisions made by a first look at something are deadly. The man who refuses to look a second time, to re-examine, to re-think, to refresh himself with the already known facts, is a fool. A second look may not change his mind but if his judgement on first beholding it was correct, a second look will reinforce and deepen his conviction, and vice-versa.

May 22

They loved not their lives unto the death (They held not their lives cheap)
REVELATION 12:11

Persecution of the Christians during the reign of Marcus Aurelius was very bitter. The Emperor himself decreed the punishment of forty men who had refused to bow down to his image.

'Strip to the skin!' he commanded. They did so. 'Now go and stand on that frozen lake until you are prepared to abandon your Nazarene-God!' As the forty men took their places on the ice they lifted up their voices and sang:

'Christ, forty wrestlers have come out to wrestle for thee; to win for thee the victory; to win from thee the crown.'

After a while those standing watching noticed a disturbance among the men on the frozen lake. One man edged away, broke into a run, entered the temple, and prostrated himself before the image of the Emperor.

The captain of the guard, who had witnessed the bravery of the men and whose heart had been touched by their teachings, tore off his helmet, threw down his spear, and disrobing himself, took the place of the man who had weakened. The compensation was not slow in coming, for as the dawn broke there were forty corpses on the ice.

'Who shall dream of shrinking,
By our Captain led?'

May 23

Jabez called on the God of Israel . . . Enlarge my coast
1 CHRONICLES 4:10

Adrian Lacy was as godly a young man as you could meet. Suffering from severe asthma he lived his life under much stress, but calmly served the Lord Jesus with a steady consistent witness and testimony. He died tragically at the age of 26.

About a year before he died I received from him this message which is mine for you today:

So Jabez prayed; and his second petition was 'enlarge me'. What a good prayer this is for us today — 'and enlarge my coast'. We should desire, as Jabez did, a greater vision and a broader outlook. We have our own little circles, but let us enlarge our coasts and our borders and look farther afield. Have we not the thought of evangelization here? There are many believers today who are like the rich man of whom our Lord spoke in Luke 16, enjoying the good things that God has placed upon the table of his grace, faring sumptuously every day, feeding on the word — and yet forgetting all about the beggar man outside; the beggar man under the table. It is always darker beneath a table than above, and there are plenty of dark areas outside in the world, places where there are those who would eagerly listen to the Gospel message.

May 24

O death, where is thy sting?
1 CORINTHIANS 15:55

Interviewed on his eightieth birthday, J. B. Priestley when asked about death said that he hoped to be 'popping off soon'. I froze when I read it. The week before Evel Knievel earned 2.5 million in attempting to jump the Snake River in the United States. On being asked about death, he said 'If I get splattered on the other side of the canyon I'll only be going somewhere faster where everybody else is going eventually.' I froze even more.

This attitude to death in our society, this flippancy is frightening. Death is too serious to joke about. We should all be prepared for death, for after this, the judgement.

What about the Lord's attitude to death? I know that no one was ever born like him; no one ever lived like him, but the significant thing is, nobody ever died like him. His death was different because his death defeated death. Yet when he went out to face it there was no joking, no laughing, no hilarious, pompous boasting. He was led as a lamb to the slaughter and as a sheep before her shearers is dumb, so he opened not his mouth. The Saviour knew too well the great foe that faced him and not until his blood was shed and atonement made did he cry, 'It is finished.' Then God raised him from the dead to show that death had been defeated by his dying.

Death and facing it, for the humble believer in Christ is knowing he need fear no evil for God in Christ is with him. His rod and his staff they guide him. It is only in resurrection that he can say, 'O death, where is thy sting? O grave, where is thy victory?' Then, and only then can he mock death's power.

May 25

My heart standeth in awe of thy word . . .
PSALM 119:161

Dear Derick,

I have a friend at work who says that religion is the cause of all the trouble in Ireland. He quotes as an example the religious leaders on TV who pat one another on the back and say they are brothers and then when they get to their respective platforms they rend each other. How can I reach such a person for Christ?

Sincerely, David

Dear David,

To your friend at work who says religion is the cause of all the troubles I would simply reply as far as the Biblical interpretation of the word is concerned his allegation is false. Visiting fatherless people and separation from the anti-God attitudes of men's hearts would cause no man to lift a gun and slay another. Sin certainly would, pure Scriptural religion wouldn't.

I remember being taken around King's College Chapel, Cambridge. The world famous stained glass window looked terrible from the outside; filthy black lead, uninspiring glass. Yet when I got inside the building, what a change! The window was ablaze with colour as a brilliant sun shone through. So it is with our Lord Jesus. The cross of Calvary with the blood, the agony, and suffering that he suffered there. How awful it looks but how wonderful it is. The preaching of that cross is to them that perish foolishness but to us who are saved it is the power of God. It is not practising Biblical religion from without that saves a man. It is being changed by a living Christ from within. That only comes by repentance towards God and faith in our Lord Jesus Christ.

The best way to win such a person for Christ is to show him that Christianity to you is not a religion but trusting a person. Christ in the heart and lived out in the life is the warmest, brightest, happiest, most winsome thing in the whole wide world. It even helps people to love their neighbours, and, David, that is just what love-starved Ireland needs. Now!

Derick

71

May 26

But seek ye first the kingdom of God, and his righteousness;
and all these things shall be added unto you
MATTHEW 6:33

'But seek ye first ... '

Yes, Lord, but ...

Well, there's this girl, Lord. And if I don't move now, I might lose her. Didn't you yourself say that 'It is not good that the man should be alone'? I agree with your word, Lord.

'But seek ye first ... '

Yes, Lord, but ...

Well, you don't really know what you're asking. I mean, there's a big world out there, and precious few seem even to be aware that you exist, let alone live by faith in you. And just look at your own people, Lord. How many of them live as loose to the world as you're telling me to? One in a hundred, maybe? I mean, it's scary to step out like that. Couldn't I have one of those ninety-nine other jobs?

'But made himself of no reputation, and took upon him the form of a servant, and was made in the likeness of men: And being found in fashion as a man, he humbled himself, and became obedient unto death, even the death of the cross' (Philippians 2:7, 8).

But ...

... Yes Lord!

May 27

If the root be holy, so are the branches
ROMANS 11:16

One day a man moved into a new home. Unfortunately the house had been unoccupied for a long time and the garden was unkempt, and high with weeds. The first morning when the new occupier was looking from his upstairs window into the garden he saw, among the weeds, a beautiful rose. He went to pick it but the weeds were so high he could not find it. Returning to his upstairs window he located the rose, noted landmarks near it and eventually succeeded in finding it on his second trip! As he pulled the rose from the weeds he discovered that the stem ran nine feet to its root in his neighbour's well kept garden! Look after your own life and affairs, keep a close watch upon them, be rooted and grounded in Christ's love. The result? Your life will be fruitful in Christ and your branches will run over the wall and bloom in the midst of your neighbour's weeds.

May 28

The Lord is my helper, and I will not fear what man shall do unto me
HEBREWS 13:6

Here in Northern Ireland over the last ten years many have known their share of tragedy. Constantly, in the midst of bombing and killing, Christian values have been mocked on all sides. We have had to stand at the graveside of a young lad who was horribly murdered just before he was due to leave Northern Ireland to become a missionary. I admit to thinking long, long thoughts the day they buried John.

Another friend who had his face badly injured in a bomb explosion gave me a most thought-provoking answer when asked what he thought about the whole experience.

'If God', he answered, 'can bring order out of the chaos of the Cross, he can bring order out of the chaos of my face.'

His answer is alive in me even now and he spoke those words about ten years ago. How exactly right was his answer!

May 29

Fruitful in every good work
COLOSSIANS 1:10

There lies within the heart of every Christian a deep desire to be useful for God, to leave behind something of real value.

I love the way Andrew Murray put it: 'Have you ever noticed', he writes, 'the difference between work and fruit in the Christian life? A machine can do work: only life can bear fruit. A law can compel work: only life can spontaneously

73

bring forth fruit. Work implies effort and labour: the essential idea of fruit is that it is the silent, natural, restful produce of our inner life. The connection between work and fruit is perhaps best seen in the expression, "fruitful in every good work". It is only when good works come as the fruit of the indwelling Spirit that they are acceptable to God. Under the compulsion of law and conscience, or the influence of inclination and zeal, men may be most diligent in good works, and yet find that they have but little spiritual result. Their works are man's effort instead of being the fruit of the Spirit — the restful, natural outcome of the Spirit's operation within us.'

May 30

... a time to die ...
ECCLESIASTES 3:2

'Whenever the news of his departure came, every Christian countenance was darkened with sadness. Perhaps never was the death of one, whose sole occupation had been preaching the everlasting gospel, more felt by all the saints of God in Scotland. He used to say "Live so as to be missed": and none that saw the tears that were shed over his death would have doubted that his own life had been what he recommended to others. He had not completed more than twenty-nine years when God took him.

'On the day of his burial, business was quite suspended ... the streets, and every window, from the house to the grave, were crowded ... and many a careless man felt a secret awe creep over his hardened soul as he cast his eye on the solemn spectacle. Hundreds of souls were his reward from the Lord, ere he left us; and in him have we been taught how much one man may do who will only press farther into the presence of his God, and handle more skilfully the unsearchable riches of Christ and speak more boldly for his God.'

(Andrew Bonar on the death of Robert Murray M'Cheyne.)

What, my reader, will they say of us when we are gone?

May 31

Where prayer was wont to be made
ACTS 16:13

The secret of praying is praying in secret. The soul is drawn out in prayer. Books on prayer are good but are not good enough, just as books on cooking are good but hopeless unless there is food to work on.

We must learn to pray, and we must pray to learn to pray. While sitting in a chair reading the finest book in the world on physical health, one may waste away. So we may read whole libraries about prayer, listen to a thousand sermons on prayer, marvel at the endurance of Moses, stagger at the weeping Jeremiah and still not be able to utter the ABC's of intercessory prayer. As the bullet unspent bags no game, so the prayer-heart unburdened gathers no spoil.

June 1

Master, carest thou not that we perish?
MARK 4:38

The Saviour delayed to visit the storm tossed disciples until the storm had reached a peak. He deliberately delayed on his way to the house of Jairus until the child was dead. He waited for days after the death of Lazarus before even visiting his grave. Why?

In each case Jesus made sure that it was clear to every person involved that unless he did something, all was lost. There was no loophole allowed where people could add their usual 'Ah! but this miracle can be naturally explained'. It was a clear opportunity for God to be glorified, each individual's faith to be deepened, and an unforgettable lesson to all of the power of the Saviour over nature, death and even decomposition.

Has God delayed his coming to your aid in extremity? Rejoice, because you are about to find that God's delays are not denials.

June 2

I will guide thee with mine eye
PSALM 32:8

An eye can tell a lot. There's a message conveyed in a look that a thousand words could not say.

Watch a mother pass a message to her child in a crowded room by the look in her eye. Watch the blushing bride-to-be convey love in a look when her future husband walks into the room. See the surgeon guide the nursing sister to the right instruments with the glance of his eye.

So it is with God. As you read his word, and pray to him in secret, you get to know him and soon the consciousness of his guiding eye becomes a reality. The Lord turned and looked on Peter and that was enough. Is it enough for you?

June 3

He that keepeth his mouth, keepeth his life
PROVERBS 13:3

Think of the crimes of the tongue. Dishonesty, Unkindness, Flattery, Impurity, Blasphemy, Slander, Pride, Criticism, Exaggeration, Temper, Greed, Boasting. Keep, by God's power, a twenty four hour guard on your mouth and you will keep your life. Let the guard slip, and always say what you like, or want, or feel like, and you will lose your life.

June 4

Who did no sin, neither was guile found in his mouth
1 PETER 2:22

Ulster is full of characters and Willie Johnston (of Portadown) is one of them. I have heard him at eighty years of age preach like a young fellow with such verve, enthusiasm, and love for the Lord Jesus that it put most of us younger 'fry' to shame. Like all characters Willie Johnston has his sayings and once, when I went to conduct the funeral service of a friend, I happened upon one of them.

76

After the service we were all at the home of the bereaved having something to eat. Willie Johnston began to say how important it was to preach Christ at such a time, especially at the graveside. 'I hope', he said, 'when people come to my funeral they will know they are at the right one! I hope what the preacher says about me will be the fellow they knew! Better to preach Christ, then no fault can be found.'

Often my mind turns to Willie Johnston's quaint way of putting a very profound truth. Leave judgement to God. Preach Christ because no man has ever, or can ever, find a flaw in him.

June 5

There wrestled a man with him until the breaking of the day
GENESIS 32:24

> Make me a captive, Lord,
> And then I shall be free,
> Force me to render up my sword,
> And I shall conqueror be.
> I sink in life's alarms
> When by myself I stand;
> Imprison me within thine arms,
> And strong shall be my hand.

George Matheson

June 6

Without faith it is impossible to please him
HEBREWS 11:6

You may have been called upon to face a situation which requires great faith. You have to face the unknown with a resolve that could be summed up in Luther's Doubters' Prayer:

Lord, although I am sure of my position, I am unable to sustain it without thee. Help me, or I am lost.

You can be sure, as you face the future and the challenge of this circumstance, that the greater the faith you exercise, the more pleasure God will receive from your life. God gets no pleasure out of our service for him when we act as if we did not need him. He loves to be trusted. He is delighted when we are cast upon him. He is a jealous God, and without faith it is impossible to please him. So, lean hard on him today, it will bring him pleasure and eternal blessing to you.

June 7

Father, forgive them; for they know not what they do
LUKE 23:34

Everyone says forgiveness is a lovely idea,
Until they have something to forgive.

C. S. Lewis

June 8

Then they that gladly received his word were baptised
ACTS 2:41

Are you an unbaptised believer? I humbly submit to you that if you are, then you are disobeying your Lord. It is clear that baptism of believers is commanded by Christ as an outward symbol of what has already taken place within. It would be a strange girl who was ashamed to wear a wedding ring because she was ashamed to let the world know that she was now joined to the one she loved. Is your refusal to be baptised as a believer any different?

78

June 9

I know not the day of my death
GENESIS 27:2

It is a sober thought that this could be the last day of your life. I often remember a line of F. W. Boreham's which always pulls me up with a start:

'Wherefore let every man who has a letter to write, write it as soon as the urge falls upon him; and let him take pains to write such a letter as he would like his friend to be reading whilst the hand that inscribed it was lying idle in the grave.'

June 10

My cup runneth over
PSALM 23:5

When the Saviour gives joy, it is unspeakable joy. When he gives peace, it is peace that passeth understanding. When he gives grace, it is abundant grace. When he imparts life, it is abundant life. The robe he puts on the repentant sinner is the best robe. When he fills the cup of salvation, it runneth over. Who would enter any other fold? Who would live under any other shepherd? You? If you dwell in Satan's flock then remember that your 'shepherd' wills only to damn your soul. By the grace of God, change shepherds today for only in the Saviour's fold is there good measure, pressed down; and running over.

June 11

Whosoever looketh on a woman to lust after her hath committed adultery with her already in his heart
MATTHEW 5:28

We in the West live in a pornographic infested society. The Christian man must not be tricked into the subtle habit of the natural man who treats a woman as a thing, simply to be thrown away, once used. A woman is someone to have and to hold in God's plan of Christian marriage. Having and holding require all the virtues of Christian manhood.

June 12

Your Father knoweth what things ye have need of, before ye ask him
MATTHEW 6:8

'*I need perfume!*' sighs the violet.
'*I need flavour!*' says the peach.
'*I need colour!*' cries the poppy.
'*I need beauty!*' whispers the rose.

Here comes the sun, now filtering, now pouring through the clouds, giving perfume, flavour, colour and beauty to each as needed. So, through the Lord Jesus, the Sun of Righteousness, I have all I need.

June 13

Whom do men say that I . . . am?
MATTHEW 16:13

To the artist he is the altogether lovely one.
To the architect he is the chief corner stone.
To the baker he is the living bread.
To the banker he is the hidden treasure.
To the farmer he is the Lord of the harvest.
To the editor he is the good tidings of great joy.
To the printer he is the true type.
To the jeweller he is the pearl of great price.
To me? Everything!
To you . . . ?

June 14

Lead me in the way everlasting
PSALM 139:24

Notice how God leads. A stray 'donkey' guided Saul to a feast where he was anointed King. A king's sleepless night, the story of Esther tells us, led to the saving of a nation. David's taking of some food to his brothers led to the defeat of Goliath, the routing of the Philistines, and the eventual

80

return of the Ark to Jerusalem. A hole in the ground saved Joseph from death and led him to becoming the most powerful person in Egypt, next to Pharaoh.

It is the tiny things in life which God uses. Like opening a door. Like crossing a street. Like meeting a stranger. Like the advice of a friend. Watch the little things in your life today for 'great oaks out of little acorns grow'.

June 15

The driving is like the driving of Jehu ... for he driveth furiously
2 KINGS 9:20

Every year traffic accidents in Europe cause around 65,000 deaths and injure 1,500,000. A Los Angeles preacher suggests that these hymns should be hummed by all motorists with the speed urge:

at 65 m.p.h. — 'I'm but a stranger here. Heaven is my home'
at 75 m.p.h. — 'Nearer my God to thee'
at 85 m.p.h. — 'When the roll is called up yonder I'll be there'
at 95 m.p.h. — 'Lord I'm coming home'

June 16

See then that ye walk circumspectly, not as fools, but as wise
EPHESIANS 5:15

'There is', said Napoleon Bonaparte after his retreat from Moscow, 'only one step from the sublime to the ridiculous.' How many a fallen believer has re-iterated those words. A forty year testimony can effectively be wrecked in one second's foolishness. A young life starting out for God with such promise ends in forced silence and obscurity. For little birds there are little traps. There is just no word to describe the tragedy of it. Just one step in the wrong direction today and you may *pray* tomorrow will never come.

June 17

Give me neither poverty nor riches
PROVERBS 30:8

Have you ever met, excuse the cliche, a 'nice' person? They are so 'nice' that your senses are alerted and before long you find out they are so nice that they are nasty.

Have you ever met a seemingly righteous man? You discover before long that he is so 'righteous' he is unfair.

Have you ever met a 'free thinker'? You discover before long he is the biggest bigot you have ever come across.

The Christian should ever seek to be balanced because too far East is West.

June 18

Doth a fountain send forth at the same place sweet water and bitter
JAMES 3:11

Have you noticed the closer you walk with God the less you want to walk with the world? If Christ is sweet to you, sin is always bitter. If you know this experience then let nothing disturb that walk and nothing sour that sweetness.

June 19

Preach the word
2 TIMOTHY 4:2

Often this text is used as a right-wing evangelical threat! It is as though you grit your teeth, clench your fists and prepare for a fight. 'Preach the word, or else!'

It was certainly never meant to be that. The Christian must preach the word if the fruits of the Spirit are to be seen: love, joy, peace, long-suffering, goodness, faith, meekness, temperance. One must preach the word, simply because there is none other. See a man under the power of the Spirit preaching the word and you will see people bend under it as a field of wheat bends all in the same direction before the wind. Preach the word, not because you are forced to but because if you do not, all is lost.

June 20

I shall go to him, but he shall not return to me
2 SAMUEL 12:23

I talked one day to a lady whose little boy had died. First she had felt tremendous resentment against God. She stopped going to Christian meetings and vowed that never again would she return. Time, they say, is a great healer but whoever 'they' were 'they' did not say how much time it takes to heal. With some it takes a long time. Slowly, day after day, this Christian woman discovered that God had a great purpose in it all. The child would not come to her, the Bible said, she would go to him. Like many with a broken heart, she actually discovered God in a way she had never known him before.

June 21

His name shall be in their foreheads
REVELATION 22:4

'Who will write his name in their foreheads, grandfather?' asked the little girl. 'Why, they will write it themselves,' he answered. And it is true. Serve Jealousy and his name will be written on your very expression. Serve Ambition and as you hurry up its ladder, Ambition will stamp your every move. Serve the world and your future glances, your fawning and flattery, your pathetic 'facing-both-ways' expression will be written on your dial. Serve the Lord Jesus and his name will be written on your forehead. You write it yourself.

June 22

Where are the nine?
LUKE 17:17

Only one came back to say thank you. The other nine forgot the Saviour who had changed their lives from sickness to health, from darkness to light. It has seldom been any different. Israel forgot the kindness of God again and again. They became ungrateful, which is another way of saying that the words, 'Thank you, Lord' were forgotten. Look at the pride and arrogance it all led to! In the New Testament church the Corinthians had to be reminded by Paul that what they possessed they had been *given*. They had forgotten that!

June 23

Men ought always to pray, and not to faint
LUKE 18:1

Mr and Mrs Faithful Prayer-meeting died recently at Neglectville, in the state of Worldliness. They were born many years ago in the midst of revival fires.

Mr and Mrs Prayer-meeting had lived a notable life until recent years. But for some time now they have been confined to their home, because of 'business engagements' and severe attacks of 'fatigue and nervousness'. These symptoms were always more noticeable on prayer meeting nights. They complained of stiffness of the knees, a relaxed voice and coldness of heart. Inactivity, weakness of will (marked by much wandering of thoughts) and generally diminished vitality marked the last stage of their illness.

Their decease was accompanied by much groaning over the 'good old days' of their early life, but only a few stood by them in their last struggles.

They leave to mourn their loss many meetings and assemblies, preachers and official dignitaries, also unnumbered Christless souls outside the pale of the Church, who often sought their help in time of trouble.

Their remains will be taken before the judgment seat of Christ, where the searcher of all things will inquire into the real cause of the untimely death of so worthy a servant. It is suspected that treachery on the part of their caretakers and professed admirers will be discovered as being responsible.

June 24

I press toward the mark for the prize of the high calling of God in Christ Jesus
PHILIPPIANS 3:14

Constantly people start out on some great project with the very highest purpose in mind. They want to win children for Christ, or communicate the gospel to alcoholics, or teach the scriptures to the deaf and dumb. Then problems arise. The project very often founders on some small detail that diverts them.

Paul certainly had found the secret of all effective work for God — he kept the prize of the high calling of God in Christ Jesus ever in mind. Then he was able to press on toward the mark despite beatings, imprisonments, criticism, slander and even shipwreck.

Step back a little from the problems that surround you, and ask yourself, 'Just what am I trying to achieve?' If you have been called by God to do something, keep that calling ever in mind and soon you will be able to see the wood, despite the trees!

June 25

He leadeth me . . . for his name's sake
PSALM 23:3

For his name's sake. There is a lot in that statement for if he does not lead me in the paths of righteousness then his name is at stake. His name is the guarantee!

85

Think of his name: Wonderful!
                     Counsellor!
                     The mighty God!
                     The everlasting Father!
                     The Prince of Peace!
                     The light of the world!
                     The bread of life!
                     The good shepherd!

For his name's sake is the promise and there is, in all the universe, no greater name than his. Let *him* lead.

June 26

. . . and he made the stars also
GENESIS 1:16

I settled down in the Planetarium and watched, mesmerised, as we were taken on a journey through space.

Relationships between Time and Space were incredible. Travelling at 186,000 miles per second it would take us 100,000 years to reach the first star, we were told. And there were billions of them.

The moon, the earth, the sea, night and day, were all his great creation and then, Genesis adds, just as an aside 'and he made the stars also'.

Why should I ever careful be since such a God is mine? He will be able to make the problems and the trials of this day work together for good. He specializes in things thought impossible — after all, he made the stars.

As the journey continued I felt a great sense of worship flow over me. The God who made all of this was my friend. He loved me so much he gave his Son to die for me! I bowed my head and worshipped.

86

June 27

These six things doth the Lord hate: yea, seven are an abomination unto him:
PROVERBS 6:16

God is love, but the Bible teaches us that God also hates.

1. *A proud look* Pride comes first in this list because it is at the bottom of most sins. Compare the look of Mary and the look of Simon the Pharisee in Luke 7. Is it any wonder the Lord hates the proud look? As a man thinketh in his heart, so is he.

2. *The lying tongue* We lie constantly with our tongues, particularly with the evil tongue of gossip and flattery.

3. *Hands that shed innocent blood* None of us are without influence. 'Be careful little hands what you do' sing the children. Let the adults sing it too and obey it.

4. *A heart that deviseth wicked imaginations* 'How does your head lie, Sir Walter?' asked Raleigh's executioner. 'It matters not how your head lies, it's how your heart lies that matters,' replied the betrayed sailor, and then died.

5. *Feet that be swift in running to mischief* We run to sin but we are often slow when it comes to going to the place of prayer or doing the will of God.

6. *A false witness that speaketh lies* Let us not say we believe one thing and do another, for there is no greater false witness than that.

7. *He that soweth discord among brethren* Always return good for evil, because sometimes even if defending yourself, you sow discord among brethren. 'Vengeance is mine, I will repay,' saith the Lord.

If you want to hate what God hates, hate these seven things!

June 28

The fear of man bringeth a snare
PROVERBS 29:25

A man who is possessed by fear often begins to persecute. Think about it.

June 29

For as often as ye eat this bread, and drink this cup, ye do shew the Lord's death till he come
1 CORINTHIANS 11:26

It is every Christian's duty to remember their Lord in the breaking of bread. Consider what it cost the Saviour to prepare you a seat at his table. It cost him slander, ridicule, false accusation, rumour, gossip, malicious charges which branded him as a glutton, a drunkard and the friend of sinners. He lost his reputation and then it cost him the shedding of his own life's blood.

He went through all that for you and yet when he asks you to sit down and remember him in the breaking of the bread and the drinking of the cup you reply 'I'm too tired this morning and anyway I don't like Mr and Mrs so and so, the singing is pathetic and, sure, I'll never be missed'. In plain truth, friend, your excuse belies your downright ingratitude.

June 30

The gift of God is eternal life through Jesus Christ our Lord
ROMANS 6:23

A little boy was invited with his school class to Buckingham Palace Gardens. Standing near a greenhouse and gazing at the luscious grapes inside he thought of his mother who was ill at home and he longed to take her some.

'Could I buy some grapes?' he asked a gentleman walking past. Immediately the gentleman called to a gardener and soon an overflowing crate of grapes lay before the boy.

'But I can't afford all this,' he said, tearfully.

'Take them, son,' replied the gardener. 'I'd take them if I were you, because the King is not in the business of selling grapes — *he gives them away!*'

'The King!' exclaimed the little boy.

'Yes, it was the King you were talking to just now,' said the gardener.

Quietly and joyfully the astounded boy took his free gift home with him.

July 1

Jesus saith unto him, If I will that he tarry till I come, what is that to thee? follow thou me
JOHN 21:22

There are people who are determined to make us all the same. Maybe God has, or is calling you to a ministry for him which others find unusual. I remind you today of a letter written by Dr Ward Hewe to Florence Nightingale:

My Dear Miss Florence,

It would be unusual, and in England whatever is unusual is thought to be unsuitable; but I say to you . . . if you have a vocation for that way of life, act up to your inspiration and you will find there is never anything unbecoming . . . in doing your duty for the good of others. Choose, go on with it, wherever it may lead you and God be with you.

. . . And he was, and the whole world knows the result.

July 2

Trust in the Lord
PROVERBS 3:5

'In all thy ways acknowledge him', continues the proverb, 'and he shall direct thy paths.' Acknowledge him! Make sure you 'check-in' with him first before you attempt your new journey, your new job, your new relationship. It is all in the

89

D

acknowledging. Then he shall direct your paths, then we shall live and do this, or that. Just like a partner in marriage likes to be recognised and their advice sought before a decision is made, so God is a jealous God and likes to be acknowledged.

July 3

Withhold not good from them to whom it is due, when it is in the power of thine hand to do it
PROVERBS 3:27

We are not robots nor are we bumblebees, living merely by instinct. We have a God-given freedom to choose. Today, somewhere at sometime, in some situation, we will be given the opportunity of doing good to someone. It may be a word of encouragement or advice, it may be to say a word for the Master, it may be merely to help, as Kipling put it, 'some lame dog over some stile', but, if it is in the power of our hand to do it, let us not withhold that good.

July 4

Drink waters out of thine own cistern, and running waters out of thine own well
PROVERBS 5:15

This text is a warning, among other things, of the danger of being too often at your neighbour's place. It is a foolish business to get into the position where with your continual coming he wearies of you and so hates you.

It is also, as the subsequent verses show, an exhortation to the husband to be fond of his wife and to love her dearly. She is the wife God in his providence has chosen for him, and if he will love to excess, let it be 'always with her love'.

The text is a great pointer to the value, where possible, of a husband and wife and their family having a home of their own. Love your parents but where possible leave them and dig your own well and drink out of your own cistern.

July 5

He that winketh with the eye causeth sorrow
PROVERBS 10:10

Watch the man who is a great winker. Watch him, for you will find him a slippery customer. As Matthew Henry put it 'The dog that bites is not always the dog that barks.' Avoid winking for it shows subtle partiality and a 'We-are-the-boys-in-the-know' attitude. We do not read of the Saviour, while among men, winking. He turned and looked on Peter.

July 6

A foolish woman is clamorous . . . she saith to him, Stolen waters are sweet . . . But he knoweth not . . . that her guests are in the depths of hell
PROVERBS 9:13-18

Who knows who may read these lines? Perhaps someone who has listened to the call of the foolish woman. Robert Burns, the Scots bard, marred his great influence in the uncontrolled desires and appetites of the flesh. How different he would have been had he known the Saviour! Read the pity in these lines of Burns:

> Pleasures are like poppies spread,
> You seize the flower, its bloom is shed,
> Or like a snow falls on the river —
> A moment white — then melt forever.

Burns, Byron and Shelley all listened to the advice of the foolish woman and Shelley died at thirty, Byron at thirty-six and Burns at thirty-seven. Do not let your life and testimony be ruined by this foolish woman because 'Many strong men have been slain by her. Her house is the way to hell, going down to the chambers of death'.

July 7

There is that scattereth, and yet increaseth
PROVERBS 11:24

At the burial service of David Livingstone in Westminster Abbey a man was heard to complain, 'I went to Canada and became a millionaire and I am unhappy and forgotten. David lost his life in Africa and his memory has become immortal.' The one who felt so disappointed was none other than Livingstone's brother! Why was he heartbroken?

Look at today's text. Scatter your life and talents, money and influence, far and wide in the service of Christ and watch God give you increase, even this very day. Withhold that life of yours and live it for yourself and watch poverty tend your every move.

July 8

He that keepeth his mouth keepeth his life
PROVERBS 13:3

I know a man who is a master at keeping his mouth. He holds a position of great influence in the life of a very large and active Christian assembly in Northern Ireland. When many in that assembly were telling me about the faults in the lives of others, I always noticed that this man went quietly on with his work for the Lord.

Notice the verse does not say 'He that keepeth his mouth shut, keepeth his life'. There are times when we must speak, but

If your lips you would keep from slips,
Five things observe with care,
Of whom you speak, to whom you speak,
And how, and when and where.

Alexander Pope the poet once described the conversation of a certain woman as, 'At every word a reputation dies'. Let no reputation die with your words but let your tongue spread far and wide the fame of the Lord Jesus.

July 9

Where no oxen are, the crib is clean; but much increase is by the strength of the ox
PROVERBS 14:4

There is the home where no furniture is scratched, no crystal cracked and where the dining-room table shines at lunch, no dropped potatoes or squashed peas. No baby hand spills milk in such a house, no romping children smash the treasured sentimental vase. The crib is clean, but empty.

There is the local church where the hymn books contain no teenage scrawlings, such as 'Liverpool rules, O.K.' on the flyleaf, where the people who come are quiet and well behaved. Yet there have been a lot of funerals there recently. They are dying out instead of reaching out. The crib is clean, but emptying.

There is the Christian life that appears so very calm. No scars appear on it from battles for the cause of Christ, no sign of the dust of the road or the weariness of service for others that brings no thanks or praise. The crib is clean, but empty.

July 10

A sound heart is the life of the flesh: but envy the rottenness of the bones
PROVERBS 14:30

Envy will destroy you. If God has given someone what seems like a more outstanding gift than you possess, so what? Will they receive a greater reward just because they have a greater gift? I tell you they will have a greater responsibility, for 'To whom much is given is much expected'. If all were evangelists, where would we find the men to pastor the sick, sorrowing, bereaved and dying? If all were pastors how would the lost hear the gospel?

'A sound heart', that is a great phrase! A heart captivated with Christ and determined to serve him only brings life to the flesh. Health, vibrancy, fluency of spirit, a literal glow, is the mark of a Christian man, woman or young person who knows nothing of the rottenness of envy.

July 11

A word spoken in due season, how good is it
PROVERBS 15:23

'Come see a man who told me all things that ever I did,' said the woman coming from the well of Jacob in Samaria. It was a word in season for because of it many believed on him there.

'And Philip preached unto him Jesus,' and Ethiopa heard the gospel.

'There is a man in Israel who could cure him of his leprosy,' said the maiden to the heartbroken first lady of Syria whose husband's skin was soon like a baby's!

'The world has yet to see what God can do with a man who is wholly dedicated to him,' said Henry Varley to D. H. Moody. 'I'll be that man,' said Moody and the late nineteenth century knew the result of that word in season.

July 12

When a man's ways please the Lord, he maketh even his enemies to be at peace with him
PROVERBS 16:7

When I was preaching in a tent in Liverpool I was privileged to meet one of that city's most famous Christians, Mr Lyttle. He is a street preacher and so noted is his work, that even the city press have featured his life story.

Mr Lyttle brought a street vendor to the tent one evening and he waited behind for a chat with me. 'That man, Mr Lyttle, you know,' said the man with a rich Liverpuddlian accent, 'was once hated by the hard men who sell on the streets — we are a tough bunch! They told him to go away, and abused him to his face. Yet he kept at it, helped us any way he could, and I'll tell you, there is no man more respected now by the street vendors than he is. They would do anything for him.'

94

July 13

Children's children are the crown of old men
PROVERBS 17:6

Grandfathers are not necessarily old men but one thing is for sure, they are getting on! Watch the look on their faces when a grandchild comes into the room, watch them renew their youth as they romp on the floor with the tiny grandchild or lend their car to the grown one.

A special place should always be given to grandfather in any family circle because the Bible clearly says they are his crown. For him they represent great fulfilment and to rob him of a place in their affections is to steal his crown.

July 14

The sluggard will not plow by reason of the cold; therefore shall he beg in harvest, and have nothing
PROVERBS 20:4

'It's too cold,' so the ploughman does not plough and later begs.

'It's too difficult,' so the local church never reaches out to the lost and none are won.

'It's too late,' thinks the hardened sinner and perishes.

'It's too controversial,' so the planned effort to use *all* means to win people remains just a planned effort and nothing comes of it.

'It's not necessary now, it can wait,' and tomorrow never comes, and, 'it' waits forever.

'It's just that he's too young,' they say, and now he's too old.

The truth is if you would have a harvest friend, you must plough now; rain, hail, sleet or snow!

July 15

It is better to dwell in a corner of the housetop, than with a brawling woman in a wide house
PROVERBS 21:9

A scolding woman! A quiet rooftop corner is a veritable paradise from such a tongue. On Belfast streets I have seen a well-armed regiment run from a crowd of scolding women in their fury. Anger is full-grown at birth but when a woman gives birth to it a beautiful, spacious house is no comfort! If you come across her, marry her not, lads. Safer the bed-sitter flat of bachelorhood than the bawling of a woman in a wide house. I'm glad to say I have *not* had to retire to the housetop as yet!

July 16

The fear of the Lord tendeth to life: and he that hath it shall abide satisfied; he shall not be visited with evil
PROVERBS 19:23

The world tells us the opposite. They say that God fearing people are losing out on life, that such a life is miserable, unfulfilled, dry and empty. They are wrong.

Here, says the proverb, is a way to have abiding satisfaction. Here is a way to escape evil. Fear the Lord. Heed him in reverence. Put him first in all things. You will *never* be a loser. Fear men and such a fear will bring a snare and catch you. Fear the Lord and you will be free.

July 17

Whoso keepeth his mouth and his tongue keepeth his soul from troubles
PROVERBS 21:23

Constantly the Book of Proverbs warns about the tongue. Maybe today you are angry with someone and about to give him a piece of your mind. Maybe there is a controversial row in your family and you are being wrongly accused. Your heart may be hot and you may even be in the right. *Keep your mouth and tongue* this day! In keeping these, by the grace of God, you will keep your soul from endless strife and trouble.

July 18

Train up a child in the way he should go: and when he is old, he will not depart from it
PROVERBS 22:6

Is administering discipline to your children breaking your heart? Does training them in the admonition of the Lord seem useless? Then cast your eye over this promise in God's word. Some far distant day they will remember your training. When some unseen storm bursts on their heads they will ask: 'What would Dad have done? How would Mother have reacted?'

In a grave on a hillside a few miles from this fireside where I write today lie the earthly remains of my parents whose lives influence the pattern of my life every day I live. I have children of my own now. What my parents taught me, I teach them.

July 19

A good name is rather to be chosen than great riches, and loving favour than silver and gold
PROVERBS 22:1

It takes years of experience and practice of Christian principles before a good name is established. Gold and silver can be won and lost in a day. Not so a good name. Even when one with a good name fails and sins, his good name dies hard.

What about the neighbours? Have you a good name among them? What about business aquaintances? How does your name stand?

The Queen of Sheba heard of the fame of Solomon, 'concerning the name of the Lord'. Immediately Solomon was spoken of in her presence the name of the Lord was linked with him. Such an association brings loving favour and such is rather to be chosen than silver or gold.

July 20

The king's heart is in the hand of the Lord, as the rivers of water: he turneth it whithersoever he will
PROVERBS 21:1

Every town and hamlet, every city and community has its local king. The man in power can be quickly and easily identified. Never be afraid of him. Never.

The nations are as a drop in the bucket with the Lord: the kings are turned by him like a turning river of water. Do not cower from him: 'render therefore unto Caesar the things which are Caesar's and unto God the things that are God's.' Never worship men for they have feet of clay. Never worship or be frightened of the king — he is here today and gone tomorrow. Serve the Lord with a full heart whether the king be for it or not. His heart is in the hand of the Lord, anyway.

July 21

Whoso boasteth himself of a false gift is like clouds and wind without rain
PROVERBS 25:14

To pretend to have a gift, even to be recognised by others to have a particular talent and not to possess it, is a poor thing. Here come the clouds and wind, howling, darkening the sky but no rain falls; such is a man who boasteth himself of a false gift. All noise and all bustle but no follow-through, no substance. Better to get on with what gifts you have and refresh all around you with the God-given results of those.

> Whatever you are — be that!
> Whatever you say — be true!
> Be honest in fact,
> Be nobody else but you.

July 22

Wrath is cruel, and anger is outrageous; but who is able to stand before envy?
PROVERBS 27:4

This is a mighty proverb. Some reader whose eye it may catch may now be suffering from the miserable beggar, envy. Why is it worse than wrath or anger? It seems to me that when a man or woman is angry you can at least see that they are 'mad at something'. Envy is not so obvious. Like a cancer it may seem to be just a headache today or a twitching pain tomorrow but all the time it is the deep-seated cause of demise.

Nothing is worse than a jealous or envious man or woman. Who can stand before them? Only those who trust in the Lord and lean not to their own understanding.

July 23

As in water face answereth to face, so the heart of man to man
PROVERBS 27:19

Experience of life teaches you that your heart is the same as another's, your problems are his.

I once flew to South Korea. It took seventeen hours. Tired and weary, I had to preach the gospel by interpretation on the evening of my arrival. The subject was 'The Woman at the Well'.

No way did I really understand that as in water face answereth to face, so the heart of man to man. A Korean, listening to the story of how the needy sinful woman took a drink of the Living Water, took a drink himself! You could have blown me over like a feather when they told the story to me! Koreans or Irish, Canadians or dwellers in Katmandu have needs, desires, problems and hearts which are identical.

Preach the word to all peoples that Christ is the answer to their every need.

July 24

Most gladly therefore will I rather glory in my infirmities, that the power of Christ may rest upon me
2 CORINTHIANS 12:9

When God delivered Israel out of Egypt, he didn't send an army or an orator as we would have done. God sent a man who had been in the desert forty years, and had an impediment in his speech. It is weakness that God wants! Nothing is small when God handles it.

Dwight L. Moody

July 25

Wisdom is too high for a fool: he openeth not his mouth in the gate
PROVERBS 24:7

I was in the coffee shop one morning with my two and a half year old invariable companion, Kathryn. While she drank her invariable coke and I eased the pace with an invariable cup of coffee, we watched the madding crowd.

I began to try and fit the people into categories. An old man sat near by and I'm sure he hadn't had a bath for a month or two: a well dressed lady sat with her child: a couple of lads from work bounced in out of the cold air. Class distinction, I thought, is there such a thing?

Let me answer my own question this way. People's needs and hearts are the same but it is not what you think you are, it is what you think — you are! In other words, the character within is what a man or woman is without.

A person who is a fool at heart, 'openeth not his mouth in the gate'. You never see him make decisions and actually do great things when the leaders of the land confer (as they did in Bible times 'in the gate' of the city). Such wisdom is too high for him.

Class distinction? The distinction is between those in whose hearts the Saviour reigns and rules as Lord and those in whose heart the Prince of this world reigns.

100

July 26

Pride goeth before destruction, and an haughty spirit before a fall
PROVERBS 16:18

Think on these names and the lives associated with them. Cain, Miriam, Saul, Absalom, Ahab the publican, Simon the Pharisee, the leaders of the Church of Corinth, the Laodiceans. What had they all in common? Pride. What followed? Destruction and a fall.

Cain was a marked man to the day of his death. Miriam got leprosy. Saul committed suicide. Absalom swung by his hair in the oak. The publican, Simon the Pharisee and the Corinthian leaders have been labelled by God in his word forever. Although the Laodiceans said 'I am rich and increased with goods and have need of nothing', the Lord said, 'Thou art wretched, and miserable, and poor, and blind, and naked.'

As my father-in-law once said to me about proud men who, though talented, ruin their gift by being proud of it instead of grateful for it: 'They were great until they *discovered* that they were great!' Indeed.

July 27

Despise not thy mother when she is old
PROVERBS 23:22

'He was crying because all his wife's work and kindness to her mother had been despised,' said a friend of mine the other day, 'despised not by the old mother but by those who should have known better.'

I thought long thoughts when I heard that story. I knew what God's thoughts concerning that faithful daughter would be. It could be that you who are reading this have an aged mother on your hands. Not the easiest of problems. She can be awkward and cantankerous. Never mind: you might be worse when you reach her age! Despise her not. God knows all about the problem and will reward you, openly. Bite your tongue. Love, love and love again.

101

One day you will be glad. The wheel will turn and turn and one day your child will not despise you; will love, keep and treasure you; will need you and feed you when you're sixty-four! (Shuddering thought, isn't it?)

July 28

As cold waters to a thirsty soul, so is good news from a far country
PROVERBS 25:25

Naomi. She was in Moab, a far country. In time of famine she had fled from the land of Israel and the will of God. There is nowhere as lonely, or a spiritual condition as bitter, as being out of God's will.

Then one happy day the news came from Israel that the Lord had visited his people in giving them bread. Would she go back to God's will and plan for her life? Could she go back after failing? She must. She would. She did! Back to Bethlehem, back to God and to see her daughter-in-law marry Boaz, to love their child Obed who became the grandfather of King David whose lineage led on to the birth of the Son of King David whose lineage led on to the birth of the Son of God! Back to blessing!

Have you turned away from the God whom you once loved and served? I have good news from a far country. There is forgiveness and blessing above all that you could ask or think there for you. Prodigal, go back. Back to blessing. Go back, now!

July 29

A fool uttereth all his mind: but a wise man keepeth it in till afterwards
PROVERBS 29:11

One day while walking down Fifth Avenue in New York I chanced for the first time upon Tiffany's, the world's greatest jewellery store. I didn't know anything about

Tiffany's as I live down a quiet Irish road half-way between the sea and the countryside, but the single, staggeringly beautiful jewel in the window held my attention. It drew me in to see the tens of millions of dollars of jewellery. I even bought some of it! All of their goods were not in the shop window.

So, says the proverb, do not utter all your mind like the fool does, keep it in till afterwards. Millions of people might listen to your mind some day if you keep it in till afterwards!

'Rubbish,' you say. No, not rubbish. As Alexander Solzhenitsyn was being taken by the KGB to prison he felt like shouting to the people passing by, 'Look at what these foolish men are doing to your country. Do something!' But he thought better of it. He decided he would keep it in 'till afterwards'. Now the whole world knows through Solzhenitsyn's writings about Stalinism and its horrors. Millions listen when he speaks.

July 30

There are three things that are never satisfied, yea, four things say not, it is enough: The grave; and the barren womb; the earth that is not filled with water; and the fire that saith not, it is enough
PROVERBS 30:15, 16

The grave is never satisfied. It robs us of life. The childless woman is never satisfied with her barrenness, though even it be allowed of God. Drought must have rain or it will always groan. An unquenched fire that will never give over is a hungry, unsatisfied horror.

The grave, barrenness, drought and fire all came because of sin on the earth. In the final eternal state of the redeemed there will be no graves, all the redeemed children will be gathered in, thirst and fire will only be in Hell, never in Heaven. Is it any wonder the Christian says: 'I shall be satisfied when I awake with thy likeness'?

103

July 31

Every word of God is pure
PROVERBS 30:5

It is a staggering statement. If preachers used the word of God more in their preaching, people would truly value what they say. If Sunday School teachers poured the word of God into their pupils they could be certain that every word they teach them is worth more than anything this world can ever offer.

At the Crescent Church in Belfast I had the privilege of preaching on the six petitions of the prayer Jesus gave to his disciples as a pattern for their prayer lives. Very simple words they are. Through those words of God, one young man was gloriously converted. One hospital theatre Sister who had handed in her resignation took it back again. One young Christian who had got drunk one night when trouble surged around him was restored to his Lord and enjoyed the sweetness of forgiveness. Other people whose hearts were touched with the word kept coming to tell what God had done. Only a tiny fragment of mighty Scripture, but what a blessing! Every word pure! Learn the word of God, don't dispute it, don't debate it, believe it, live it, *stand fast*.

August 1

James, a servant of God and of our Lord Jesus Christ
JAMES 1:1

James the writer is believed by many to have been the brother of our Lord Jesus. He was called 'The Just One' and was, some say, nicknamed 'Camel Knees' because of his mighty prayer life. He could have called himself, in the opening remarks of his epistle, 'a leader of the Jerusalem Church'. He might have referred to himself using many other important names but he simply states that he is a 'servant of God and of our Lord Jesus Christ'.

What then is a servant, because the word 'serve' occurs over 1,000 times in the Bible? A servant is one who runs errands for his master. James considered himself one who constantly ran errands for his Master, and so must we. Could he call on *you* today? Would you run to answer immediately?

August 2

Count it all joy when you fall into divers temptations
JAMES 1:2

The text does not say 'if you fall into trials' it says 'when'. Temptations are sent by Satan to make the Christian stumble but trials are sent by God in order to make the Christian stand. They are for his maturity because how can a race be won without running? How can a goal be reached without striving? How can a fine sailor be made in fair weather? How can faith flourish without fire? Rejoice today if you are in a trial for 'he giveth more grace', and patience will be one of your great virtues as a result. Then you will be fully grown in the Christian life, wanting nothing.

August 3

Let him ask in faith, nothing wavering. For he that wavereth is like a wave of the sea driven with the wind and tossed
JAMES 1:6

Watch a wave against any harbour wall. It looks as though it is coming in one direction but suddenly the wind drives it in another. The man or woman in prayer who does not ask in faith is just like this. They waver and receive nothing. James in subsequent verses shows that the two great forces for *ruining* folk, poverty and riches, cannot do so to the man of faith. Poverty, if it comes, does not discourage and riches, if they come, do not corrupt and win. 'In Christ' the Christian can face *any* situation by faith.

August 4

If any man be a hearer of the word, and not a doer, he is like unto a man beholding his natural face in a glass: For he beholdeth himself, and goeth his way, and straightway forgetteth what manner of man he was

JAMES 1:23

'The greatest god ever raised to man', said the philosopher, 'was the mirror.'

Have you noticed that when you check how you look in the mirror, a few minutes later you find you have completely forgotten what you looked like and have to re-check? Some people hear God's word like that. They look at it as in a mirror but immediately forget what it has shown them about themselves.

When you look in a mirror and see that your face is dirty you go and wash in water. The unconverted man when looking into God's word should see his lost condition and run to the Saviour and his work at Calvary for forgiveness and cleansing. But he doesn't.

The Christian who on looking into the mirror of God's word and finding that God requires him to do something but simply forgets all about it, has just the same attitude as the unconverted man. He is a hearer of the word but not a doer.

August 5

If any man among you seem to be religious, and bridleth not his tongue, but deceiveth his own heart, this man's religion is vain

JAMES 1:26

To observe the external duties of faith and at the same time say what you like, to whomever you like, when you like and how you like; you might as well build a beautiful home with exquisite furniture and then go and systematically smash everything with a sledgehammer.

106

August 6

My brethren, have not the faith of our Lord Jesus Christ, the Lord of glory, with respect of persons
JAMES 2:1

We are told here how very inconsistent it is to have the faith of our Lord Jesus and yet to treat people in a certain way, not because they deserve it but for a hidden reason outside of their character. Often Christians discriminate on the basis of a person's position in the local church, or influence in the community, or how much money they have, or what school tie they wear.

How can we do such things and say we are the Lord's? Did he discriminate? Never. Look at his sinless movements amongst men. I see him save a tax collector, a fisherman, a prostitute, a leper, a ruler of the synagogue's daughter, a man who had a legion of devils in him and a man called Nathaniel in whom there was no guile. Let us be like him.

August 7

For whosoever shall keep the whole law and yet offend in one point, he is guilty of all
JAMES 2:10

When visiting South Korea, a Korean banker invited me to his home and explained that he was rather confused by the gospel message he had heard me preach. I had said we were sinners and then I pointed to a sinless Saviour. This was beyond his understanding. Confucious and Buddha were gods, but they had sinned; were there not records of their sins? He could identify with them. Yet I expected him to put his trust in a God who had sent his sinless Son to die for him? How could he ever identify with such a sinless person?

So far as I know, that Korean never trusted the Saviour, but if he had meditated on today's verse he might have. We have all broken God's law in some point and it is *because* the Saviour of sinners has never offended in one point, *because* he is sinless and therefore could die *for* our sin that we can be set free. Such is the message of the gospel. Though you are guilty of all, if you will repent and trust the Lord Jesus as your Saviour, you will be forgiven all.

August 8

If a brother or sister be naked, and destitute of daily food, and one of you say unto them 'Depart in peace, be ye warmed and filled'; notwithstanding ye give them not those things which are needful to the body; what doth it profit?
JAMES 2:15, 16

John Wesley put it this way:

'Do all the good you can, by all the means you can, in all the ways you can, in all the places you can, at all the times you can to all the people you can, as long as ever you can.'

But Charles Lamb put it this way:

'The greatest pleasure I know is to do a good action by stealth and to have it found out by accident.'

August 9

Shew me thy faith without thy works, and I will shew thee my faith by my works
JAMES 2:18

Every Christian, if his or her faith is called into question by men or the devil should be able, without hesitation, to point to his or her transformed life. If not, why not?

August 10

Seest thou how faith wrought with his (Abraham's) works, and by works was faith made perfect
JAMES 2:22

The greater the darkness the clearer the stars will shine.

August 11

I have called you friends
JOHN 15:15

Friend of Jesus. Just medidate on that for a little time today. Think of all the shades of meaning of that word 'Friend'. Compatability, on friendly relations, acquaintanceship, guest, confidant, inseparable, staunch, fast, firm, devoted, loyal, faithful, sympathetic, favoured, protected. Abraham was a friend of God. Why, I would rather have God as my friend and the whole world my enemy than God as my enemy and the whole world my friend.

August 12

But the tongue can no man tame; it is an unruly evil, full of deadly poison
JAMES 3:8

Gossip is what you say behind a person's back which you would not dare say to their face. Flattery is what you say to their face which you would never say behind their back.

August 13

The tongue is a fire
JAMES 3:6

The fire of destructive criticism is a great sin of the tongue. Before you raise your tongue to criticise another today, ask three questions, and if your criticism can pass these three tests go ahead.

    1. Is it true?
    2. Is it necessary?
    3. Is it kind?

August 14

This wisdom descendeth not from above, but is earthly, sensual, devilish. For where envying is, there is confusion and every evil work
JAMES 3:15, 16

There is a wisdom that is hatched in hell. It has the hallmarks of the unholy trinity for it is:

> Earthly — that is of 'the World'
> Sensual — that is of 'the Flesh'
> Devilish — that is of 'the Devil'

This wisdom measures everything by earth's standards. It is merely occupied with what can be seen and known by the senses and is not concerned with the spiritual. It is inspired and controlled by the devil. It poses in all sorts of forms and is so easy to accept. No faith is needed, no grasping the heavenly standard, no ridicule from men hounds the one who listens to its whisperings. Obey its dictator and the inward effect will be 'confusion' and the outward effect 'confusion and every evil work'. Ask your heart today if your decisions and plans are based on the standards of this wisdom? If so, seek cleansing.

August 15

The wisdom that is from above is first pure, then peaceable, gentle, and easy to be intreated, full of mercy and good fruits, without partiality, and without hypocrisy
JAMES 3:17

There is a wisdom that is from heaven. Its standard and results are 'pure', it brings an inward experience that is undefiled. Outwardly it makes its children peace-loving, gentle, approachable and open to reason. It knows nothing of bigotry. It is full of compassion and is not merely formal, accurate, precise, regular and loveless. It is full of kind actions, because an ounce of help is worth a ton of pity. Of course, dear to the heart of James, it is without respect of persons!

How does a person get this wisdom? Why, 'If any of you lack wisdom, let him ask of God, that giveth to all men liberally, and upbraideth not; and it shall be given him'

(Jas. 1. 5).

August 16

Ye ask, and receive not, because ye ask amiss, that ye may consume it upon your lusts
JAMES 4:3

There is that kind of request to God in prayer that always receives 'no' for an answer. It is the request that asks for something so that we might merely have the pleasure derived therefrom for the fulfilment of our own desire. We ask with a wrong purpose for there is an underlying evil, selfish motive behind the asking.

Prayer is not asking God for what we want: it is asking God for what he wants. Our asking must ever be based on the example of our Lord Jesus who prayed 'Not my will but thine be done'.

August 17

Ye adulterers and adulteresses, know ye not that the friendship of the world is enmity with God?
JAMES 4:4

If your husband or wife left you for the arms of another today, how would you feel? If their affection and love were poured into another's life to the exclusion of yours, what would you say?

The very same feeling applies to the Lord. How do you think your Lord feels when you set your affection on those things which oppose him and his word? How do you think he feels when you flirt with the world? He feels the very same way as you would if one whose love was pledged to you went and gave that love to another.

August 18

Submit yourselves therefore to God
JAMES 4:7

There is a submitting that brings freedom. It is submitting to God. To be under his sovereignty is to be free, but to give in to Satan is to be in bondage.

Here is a man condemned to be hanged under the king's law at 6 a.m. Earlier in the morning the king dies and

111

under English law the first thing a new monarch can do is to free the prisoner nearest the gallows. The new monarch exercises the prerogative of mercy and at 8 a.m. the condemned man walks out of prison a free man. What made the difference? He had changed sovereigns!

Submit yourselves therefore to God.

August 19

Speak not evil one of another, brethren
JAMES 4:11

In fifty years of Christian experience the thing I have found that caused the greatest harm was *tale bearing.*

D. E. Hoste

August 20

Go to now, ye that say, To day or to morrow we will go into such a city, and continue there a year, and buy and sell, and get gain: Whereas ye know not what shall be on the morrow
JAMES 4:13, 14

Nothing wrong with planning to go to a city. Nothing wrong with planning to continue there a year. Nothing wrong with planning to buy and sell. Nothing wrong with planning to make a profit. Yet there is *everything* wrong with all this if we do not add, 'If the Lord will.'

We must never plan to make a move and leave God out. The rich farmer that Jesus talked about was not necessarily an unconverted man. His sin was that he planned to pull down his house and build greater without acknowledging God, forgetting that he knew not what would be on the morrow, indeed not realising that that very night God required his soul.

112

August 21

Therefore to him that knoweth to do good, and doeth it not,
to him it is sin
JAMES 4:17

I expect to pass through this world but once. Any good therefore that I can do, or any kindness that I can show to any fellow creature, let me do it now. Let me not defer it or neglect it, for I shall not pass this way again.

Stephen Grellet

August 22

The cries of them . . . are entered into the ears of the Lord of
sabaoth
JAMES 5:4

I have a friend who is a policeman and a dedicated Christian. He is a driver and often has to convey prisoners from the courtroom to the prison. He tells me that men who have been convicted of crimes often get into his vehicle laughing at the lightness of their sentence. 'As I shut the door,' he tells me, 'I often say to them, "Boys! that is not the last judge you will face. There is a higher! You will have to face God one day." '

August 23

Be patient therefore, brethren, unto the coming of the Lord
JAMES 5:7

The second coming of Christ is very often preached as a threat, while everywhere in the New Testament it is preached as a comfort. The people James had in mind were under severe persecution and in order to comfort them he whispers in their ears this gracious and thrilling news no less than three times. Once in this verse, then in the next one, 'for the coming of the Lord draweth nigh' and again in the following one, 'the judge standeth before the door'.

There are 1,853 biblical references to the second coming of Christ. In the New Testament alone there are 300. Be patient today, Christian, for conduct is not influenced so much by our experience as by our expectations.

113

August 24

*The husbandman waiteth for the precious fruit of the earth,
and hath long patience for it, until he receive the early and
latter rain*
JAMES 5:7

The early rain comes in late autumn to germinate the seed.
The latter rain comes in the spring leading to the swelling of
the grain towards harvest. Patiently the farmer waits. He
could worry but it won't hurry the crop one inch. He could
hold discussions with his fellow farmers asking 'Will it?' or
'Won't it?' but discussion will not change the promise of God
about the inevitability of 'seedtime and harvest'.

So must the believer in Christ be patient and *believe*
the promises of God. What God says, *he will do*. Wait
patiently and see.

August 25

*Take, my brethren, the prophets, who have spoken in the
name of the Lord, for an example of suffering affliction, and
of patience*
JAMES 5:10

James must have been a great preacher for he certainly
knows about the art of good illustration. Here he is again
urging downhearted, persecuted believers to be patient in
their difficult circumstances. 'Take the prophets,' he says.
Indeed. Hebrews 11 tells us how they were afflicted. Cruel
mockings, scourgings, bonds, imprisonment, stoning —
some were sawn asunder, tempted, slain with the sword.
Despite their persecution, look at their patience!

Have you known one quarter of the persecution these
men suffered? As Matthew Henry puts it, 'The best men
have had the hardest usage in this world.' As you face the
persecution and ridicule of the world today for your
Christian stand, remember that they have never driven nails
through your hands and feet, yet.

August 26

Ye have heard of the patience of Job
JAMES 5:11

Job lost seven sons and three daughters. He lost all his substance and eventually his health. He went through the most unbelievable suffering, with men, his wife and friends turning against him. What always amazes me about God's dealings is that God, in his sovereign will, allowed all this to happen. Yet there is absolutely no mention, anywhere, that God ever gave Job an explanation as to why it all happened to him. The clear indication is that Job was a better man at the end of his experiences than he was at the beginning, but he became such a man without any explanation from God! It seems to me that once you have heard God's voice (as Job obviously had in his earlier days) you can bear his silences.

August 27

Is any among you afflicted? let him pray. Is any merry? let him sing psalms
JAMES 5:13

When the world is on top of you ... pray!
When you are on top of the world ... praise!
John Blanchard

August 28

The effectual fervent prayer of a righteous man availeth much
JAMES 5:16

What a man is on his knees before God,
That he is — and nothing more.
Robert Murray M'Cheyne

115

August 29

And he (Elijah) . . . prayed again
JAMES 5:17

If your troubles are deep-seated or longstanding,
Try kneeling.

August 30

Go ye therefore, and teach all nations
MATTHEW 28:19

O, the value of winning souls! O, the sheer unbelievable thrill of telling folk about Christ and seeing them believe in him and have a multitude of sins hidden! What greater work could any mortal man or woman, boy or girl engage in? Not only does it bring great blessing, but while a Christian is busy winning souls, he has no time for fooling about with sin.

September 1

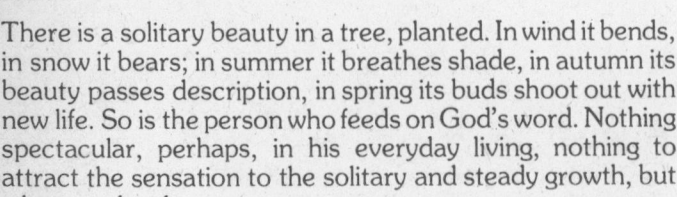

His delight is in the law of the Lord . . . he shall be like a tree planted . . .
PSALM 1:2, 3
The ungodly . . . are like the chaff which the wind driveth away
PSALM 1:4

There is a solitary beauty in a tree, planted. In wind it bends, in snow it bears; in summer it breathes shade, in autumn its beauty passes description, in spring its buds shoot out with new life. So is the person who feeds on God's word. Nothing spectacular, perhaps, in his everyday living, nothing to attract the sensation to the solitary and steady growth, but whatever he does prospers.

The ungodly are like the chaff. They abound in multitudes but one whiff of wind and they are gone; they simply perish.

Which would you rather be: chaff or a tree planted?

September 2

The eyes of a fool are in the ends of the earth
PROVERBS 17:24

This does not mean that we must not be interested in the ends of the earth for the gospel's sake but it means we must not treat things contemptuously simply because they are homely and near at hand. Always remember the lines:

> 'Each man's chimney is his Golden Milestone,
> Is the central point from which he measures every
>   distance.'

September 3

. . . a vapour that appeareth for a little time
JAMES 4:14

> Life is too short to waste,
> In critic peep or cynic bark,
> Quarrel, or reprimand,
> 'Twill soon be dark;
> Up! Mind thine own aim, and
> God speed the mark!

R. W. Emerson

September 4

. . . lest ye forget
DEUTERONOMY 4:23

> If, drunk with sight of power, we loose
> Wild tongues that have not thee in awe,
> Such boastings as the Gentiles use,
> Or lesser breeds without the law —
> Lord God of Hosts, be with us yet,
> Lest we forget — lest we forget!

Rudyard Kipling

117

September 5

My strength is made perfect in weakness
2 CORINTHIANS 12:9

The other day came the news of the death of a little three-year-old girl. She had just had a very big heart operation and the surgeon had said that of the several children who were having the same operation only seventy five per cent would survive.

When the news of the death of her child was broken to the Christian mother, she spoke what I think were the bravest words possible: 'He took our little girl because he knew we could bear it.'

Such words do more for me than all the 'sermons' I have ever listened to. They touch something that is as deep as the promises of God.

September 6

Boast not thyself of to morrow; for thou knowest not what a day may bring forth
PROVERBS 27:1

On June 23rd 1914   Austria sent an ultimatum to Serbia.

On June 28th 1914   Austria declared war on Serbia.

On August 1st 1914   Germany declared war on Russia.

On August 3rd 1914   Germany declared war on France.

On August 4th 1914   Britain declared war on Germany.

By 1918 8,530,000 were killed and 21,205,000 were wounded.

118

September 7

She . . . brought an alabaster box of ointment . . . and kissed his feet, and anointed them with the ointment
LUKE 7:37,38

Talk not of wasted affection, affection never was wasted;
If it enrich not the heart of another, its waters, returning
Back to their springs, like the rain, shall fill them full of refreshment.

That which the fountain sends forth returns again to the fountain.

Longfellow

September 8

Thine eyes did see my substance, yet being imperfect; and in thy book all my members were written . . . when as yet there was none of them
PSALM 139:16

There is no end to man's ingenuity. Dr Clemts introduced the craze of 'Womb Music', where music is played to the yet unborn child. She claims that Brahms makes their toes curl!

Despite man's attempts at influencing children yet unborn the wonder of God's creation cannot be erased. God had written down all your members, the colour of your eyes, the number of hairs in your head, right handedness or left handedness, and everything else about them 'when as yet there was none of them'.

The child that is yet to be? God's eyes sees his substance already, and by his grace, great things are in store.

September 9

I will not fail . . .
JOSHUA 1:5

There was a belief at the turn of this century that education, intelligence and science could be easily substituted for a belief in God. Have such things succeeded? Not at all. They

119

have all failed and the result is that never before has there been such brilliantly educated godlessness, boredom, crime and immorality. It is still true amidst all the failures of mere men and their wisdom — *he shall not fail.*

Trust him today.

September 10

He that sounded the trumpet was by me
NEHEMIAH 4:18

A fierce host was gathering against Nehemiah because of his great work for God. 'They shall not know, neither see, till we come in the midst among them, and slay them, and cause the work to cease,' they cried. The wall of Jerusalem was now half raised but the enemy were determined to prevent any further work on it.

The leader rose up in the midst of God's discouraged people and became the rallying point for his whole army of builders. 'He that sounded the trumpet was by me,' says Nehemiah. Think of the sight this little phrase describes.

Nehemiah hurries up and down his half completed wall because those who were working were separated one far from another. When there is a threat to one section of the wall he gets his trumpeter to sound out his trumpet and help rushes to the section under threat from the enemy.

Who knows what you will see before this day is through? Will you sound a trumpet? Will you call God's people's attention to the need? Will you encourage the discouraged and remind them of the faithfulness of God?

September 11

... In singleness of heart ...
COLOSSIANS 3:22

It is best not to swap horses while crossing the river.
Abraham Lincoln

September 12

What think ye of Christ?
MATTHEW 22:42

Test all men by this question. Mark carefully their reaction.
Their answers will amaze you.

'Oh, he was a good man.'

'I think he could have been the Son of God.'

'His death was a mistake, was it not?'

'I'm not certain about his miracles.'

Each individual answer will usually tell you the spiritual
condition of the person you question. This question is the
whole basis of *everything*. It is the most important question
in the whole universe. What is your answer? Upon it
depends your place in eternity, your spiritual state now and
the exact relationship you have with God. It is no trite,
outworn evangelical phrase — there is life and death in it.

What think ye of Christ? Is the test

To try both your state and your scheme

You cannot be right in the rest

Unless you think rightly of him.

September 13

. . . He is risen
MARK 16:6

We have all heard many arguments in our time against the
resurrection. Intellectuals, academics and a million other
men have raised their seemingly clever objections to the
bodily resurrection of the Son of God from the dead. They
say the disciples spread this truth as a lie to cover up Christ's
defeat.

Yet, there is one truth that they all seem to be afraid
of. It always stumps them. It is the fact that men do not lay
down their lives willingly for a lie. No one ever laid down his
life in Asia or in Africa to translate Plato or Aristotle, Kant or
Hegel, Shakespeare or Milton, but hundreds have done so
to carry God's word to the ends of the earth. It is a fact that
every single apostle (apart from John) died an unnatural
death because of their belief in the resurrection of Jesus
Christ.

Proof indeed!

121

E

September 14

Whoso offereth praise glorifieth me
PSALM 50:23

It was a beautiful autumn day and my friend Eric Palethorpe drove me for a memorable visit to the city of York. We went round all the many historical sites and ambled through the famous 'Shambles' where the beautiful shops belie the name of the district in which they stand.

Suddenly I noticed a shop with a handsomely inscribed text above the door. To my surprise the shop was given over to selling tastefully inscribed Bible texts and cards. I just had to go in. There was an old lady behind the counter and no sooner had we entered the shop than she cheerfully asked: 'Are you believers?' We were delighted to be able to say that we were, whereupon, with a twinkle in her eye, the old lady leaned over the counter and said:

'It is worth a King's ransom to be able to say HALLELUJAH!'

September 15

Take now thy son, thine only son Isaac . . . and offer him there
GENESIS 22:2

If it had been your son or mine, what would your reaction have been to such a request? Did Abraham obey without any reason? *No.* His faith was a blind faith as far as obedience was concerned but as to *why* he obeyed God at all, his faith was not in the least blind.

It was because Abraham knew who God was that he could trust him. It was because he was not in the dark about God that he could walk in the dark about Isaac. So, despite the unknown future facing you today, trust the God that you know through our Lord Jesus Christ.

September 16

My heart is fixed
PSALM 57:7

I am sure that in your walk every day you are aware that men treat morality not by conviction but by its usefulness in any given situation. They do not ask: 'Is it true?' they ask: 'How will it sell?' They do not ask: 'Is faith unchanging?'; they rather ask: 'Is it fashionable?' When fashions or times change then these people change too.

For the believer success is not the act of compromise. The believer's heart is fixed and his prayer is Martin Luther's:

'My conscience is taken capture by God's word. I cannot and will not recant anything. On this I take my stand. I can do no other. So help me God.'

September 17

Bring them up in the nurture and admonition of the Lord
EPHESIANS 6:4

You are probably aware of the place given to teaching comparative religion in schools. Children are taught the rudiments of every creed and philosophy and the idea is they will then choose for themselves which one to follow. It sounds grand but it is very dangerous.

One day a well-known Deist visited Samuel Taylor Coleridge, the poet. The Deist vigorously protested against the wickedness of giving theological instruction to the young.

'Consider', said he, 'the helplessness of a pastor's child. How selfish is the parent who stamps his ideas and religious prejudices into the receptive nature, as a moulder stamps the hot iron with his image! I shall prejudice my children neither for Christianity nor for Buddhism, but allow them to wait for their mature years and then choose for themselves.'

Continuing the conversation in the garden a little later, Coleridge suddenly exclaimed:

'The time was when I killed the young weeds in April and put my beds out to vegetables, flowers, and fruits. But I have now decided to permit the garden to go until August or September and then allow the beds to choose for themselves between weeds and fruit. I am unwilling to prejudice the soil either toward thistles and weeds or roses and violets.'

The lesson was obvious.

September 18

Lo, these are the outskirts of his ways: and how little a portion is heard of him? but the thunder of his power who can understand?
JOB 26:14

God whispers at times. He whispers in the conscience of the gossip, or the soul of some unscrupulous businessman. He whispers in the ear of some young man bent on impurity. What does his whisper say?

> It says that right is right;
> That it is not good to lie;
> That love is better than spite;
> And a neighbour than a spy.

God never sends a flood if a shower will do; never sends a fortune if a shilling will do; never sends an army if a man will do. And he never thunders if a whisper will do. He never gives special dreams, or voices, or visions if Scripture will do. He never works miracles if he can achieve the same end by the instrumentality of natural laws.

September 19

And I gave thee thy master's house, and thy master's wives into thy bosom, and gave thee the house of Israel and of Judah; and if that had been too little, I would moreover have given unto thee such and such things.
Wherefore hast thou despised the commandment of the Lord?

2 SAMUEL 12:8, 9

We always seem to have a sneaking suspicion in the back of our minds that there is more to be had in the wear and tear of life than that which God in his wisdom gives us. The world has a miserable expression for it. It is called 'a little on the side'.

David gave in to this lie from the pit of hell. It caused him to murder a man by placing him deliberately at the forefront of a battle; it caused him the wrath of God, and the death of the child brought into the world through his sin; it caused God's people the ridicule and laughter of the enemies of the Lord; and it has caused the sneer of sinners down through the centuries. When I was trying to point some tough teenage lads to Christ recently, they threw 'What-about-David-then?' back in my teeth.

Are you tempted to step out of the path of purity and obedience to God's commandments? Are you listening to Satan's lie that there is more enjoyment than that which God allows? Don't!

September 20

He that handleth a matter wisely shall find good
PROVERBS 16:20

A courtroom in any town or city is an amazing place to be. Drama unfolds from the witness box which fiction could never match.

Few dramas could equal the one described in this extract taken from a poem. There is a very clear message in the story but this time it came from the judge's bench. In his summing up the judge addressed the jury and said:

125

'. . . when you're in that jury room,
Remember there, and then,
That for every fallen woman
There are a hundred fallen men.
Before you render a verdict,
On what this girl has done,
Remember there's a man to blame
And that man might be your son.
This is my story, my testimony stands,
This girl is my own daughter,
And the case is in your hands.'

September 21

Let him that thinketh he standeth take heed lest he fall
1 CORINTHIANS 10:12

I was, in Ulster lingo, 'Up the Shankill'. The media call this
area of Belfast a 'Protestant stronghold' but on this
particular evening it was a stronghold of wild, untameable
children. For six nights the children's meetings had gone
well. The Lord was with us. The children sang choruses with
ardour and dash, and scripture texts and stories were
deeply implanted in young minds. The wind was behind us.

The wind suddenly changed direction that evening.
Nothing went right. The children were restless, beyond
control, and then it happened. I lost my temper. I took out
my frustrations on the teenager nearest at hand and more or
less 'threw' her out of the meeting. Ungraciously. I knew I
had grieved the Holy Spirit with my behaviour. Driving
home afterwards I 'overhauled' the meeting a dozen times
and a sneaking suspicion began to dawn on me. It had been a
busy, constantly interrupted day and I had gone to the
meeting unprepared.

Making a promise to the Lord I went to the children's
mission the following evening as Campbell Morgan put it,
'Prepared as if there were no Holy Spirit and then preaching
as if I'd never prepared.' The children listened to the
organised, prepared material, spellbound.

Going out of the meeting that night I heard an earnest Christian worker say, 'The Devil came in last night.' Yes, I thought, he came in through a careless, unprepared evangelist — 'me'.

September 22

Man is born unto trouble, as the sparks fly upward
JOB 5:7

Over the next two days we shall explore a strange and difficult truth. It is that the greatest riches in life usually come out of suffering. Today I shall concentrate on what may, to some, appear to be secular.

Beethoven spent his youth in poverty and misery. He was generally referred to as an ugly man, and tragedy of tragedies, he went stone-deaf. Not once, however, did he allow his infirmity to interfere with what he felt he was destined to accomplish — 9 symphonies, 32 piano sonatas, 17 string quartets amongst a host of other works.

Handel had first to play the clarichord in an attic in case his father found out. Later in life, he composed his most widely known work, 'The Messiah', under a cloud of misfortune and bitter disappointment. His last two operas had failed. Finally he went blind, but he refused to give in, playing from memory.

Tchaikovsky had moods that alternated between happy exuberance and black depression (Who of us haven't?) He married a girl whom he did not love because he was afraid she would commit suicide if he refused her. After nine weeks they separated and Tchaikovsky suffered such mental torture he became unconscious. Although he said he was 'worn out' and 'done for', he was conceiving in his mind the haunting and beautiful 'Pathetic' symphony.

The message is indeed clear, our 'sweetest songs are those of saddest thought'.

Do not think that you are alone in facing insurmountable problems.

127

September 23

If we suffer, we shall also reign with him
2 TIMOTHY 2:12

If great things can be produced in the secular out of great suffering; what of the spiritual? Trace the history of God's dealings with men. Did Moses come to victory easily? What of his own personal failure in slaying the Egyptian? What of Pharoah's twelve refusals to let Israel go? Were there not many tears along the way?

What of Abraham leaving the ambitious Lot to the well-watered plains? Do you think that was easy? What of Ruth gleaning corn, or Esther weeping to the King on behalf of the persecution of her people, or Nehemiah getting criticised for rebuilding Jerusalem, or Paul lashed and bleeding and left 'half-dead' in Philippi, or Timothy despised for his youth, or Calvary itself? Anywhere you look in the Scriptures greatness begins with suffering. God uses it to draw men and women to himself.

Despite the problem, God's power is greater. He can do impossible things. He can bring good out of seeming evil. All God's success stories begin with tragedies.

September 24

As we have therefore opportunity, let us do good unto all men
GALATIANS 6:10

Mend a quarrel. Search out a forgotten friend. Dismiss suspicion and replace it with trust. Write a love letter. Share some treasure. Give a soft answer. Encourage youth. Manifest your loyalty in a word or deed.

Keep a promise. Forego a grudge. Forgive an enemy. Listen. Apologize if you were wrong. Try to understand. Flout envy. Examine your demands on others. Think just of someone else. Appreciate, be kind, be gentle. Laugh a little more.

Deserve confidence. Take up arms against malice. Deny complacency. Express your gratitude. Worship your God. Gladden the heart of a child. Take pleasure in the beauty and wonder of earth. Speak your love. Speak it again. Speak it still again. Speak it still once again.

128

September 25

Do it, heartily, as to the Lord
COLOSSIANS 3:23

Have you heard about the Negro engineer who sat in the doorway of the engine room of a tiny tugboat on a southern river reading his Bible?

Since the engineer was new to him, a captain passing by stopped to chat. He noticed that the usual smells characteristic of the engine room of this particular tugboat were no longer there. The engine itself gleamed and shone. Bilge water was missing from under the engine seat. The captain was so impressed with the new order of things that he asked the engineer how he had managed it.

'Cap'n,' he said, nodding affectionately in the direction of the engine, 'it's just this way: I got a glory.'

You see, making that engine the best on the river was his glory in life and having a glory he had everything. Let's get ourselves a glory and in the words of Archibald Rutledge who told the story, 'Give it the strength we might otherwise spend in despair.'

September 26

Adam knew his wife again; and she bare a son, and called his name Seth: For God, said she, hath appointed me another seed instead of Abel whom Cain slew
GENESIS 4:25

Abel had been a young man of faith (see Heb. 11) and faith is infectious. It inspires a vision for things which unbelief and despair never do. Others catch the spirit of it. Eve, the one we berate for her disobedience, did not backslide all her days and she did not want great faith like Abel's to go

129

unperpetuated. She claimed Seth for the Lord and the Bible says that at the time of Seth's son, Enos, men began to 'Call upon the name of the Lord' (Gen. 4:26). We have the very first mention of prayer in the Bible in the godly time of Seth.

It is interesting to note that the seventh generation from Cain was the blasphemer, Lamech, but that the seventh generation from Seth was Enoch, who walked with God.

The promises of God are packed in his storehouse — open the door, Christian, and take what you want. If Eve could exercise faith, so can you.

September 27

And Caleb stilled the people . . . and said, Let us go up at once . . . But the men . . . said, We be not able to go up against the people; . . . for they are stronger than we
NUMBERS 13:30, 31

When things go wrong, as they sometimes will,
When the road you're trudging seems uphill,
When the funds are low and the debts are high,
And you want to smile, but you have to sigh.
When care is pressing you down a bit,
Rest if you must, but don't you quit.

Life is queer with its twists and turns,
As everyone of us sometimes learns,
And many a failure turns about,
When he might have won had he stuck it out.
Don't give up though the pace seems slow —
You may succeed with another blow!

Success is failure turned inside out —
The silver tint of the clouds of doubt,
And you never can tell just how close you are,
It may be near when it seems so far.
So stick to the fight when you're hardest hit,
It's when things seem worse that you must not quit.
Author unknown

September 28

And Samuel said to Saul ... Thy kingdom shall not continue: the Lord hath sought him a man after his own heart
1 SAMUEL 13:13, 14

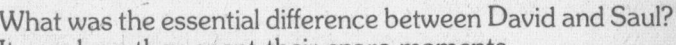

What was the essential difference between David and Saul? It was how they spent their spare moments.

The prophet Samuel did not arrive at the appointed time so Saul rushed on and offered up a burnt offering instead of waiting for Samuel to do it. Impatience. It is a deadly trait in a character, the undoing of many a life and career. The Lord took the kingdom from Saul for disobedience brought about by impatience.

When Saul's star was falling, David's was rising. Impatience had not ruled his youth, he had learned to meditate upon God's word day and night as he looked after his father's sheep. Spare moments were responsible for David's blessing in his youth. We must never forget, however, that the reason why David won in his youth later caused his defeat. It was the wasted spare moments when he was a man that caused David's greatest sin when he was King of Israel.

What are you when you are alone? How are those spare moments spent?

September 29

My soul, wait thou only upon God
PSALM 62:5

I faced a dilemma. I had to speak from a particular passage of Scripture, before a very eager and spiritually hungry congregation. I did not fully understand the passage and for two days had wrestled with the interpretation.

Before going into the pulpit I met with three men to pray. It was not easy to pray. My spirit was uninspired. I was frightened of not rightly dividing the word of truth. So we prayed on. Waiting, waiting, and waiting upon God.

131

Suddenly we broke through. That is the only way I can describe it. The assurance of God's help and promise of blessing were so real in my soul that we were praising God right there for what he was going to do. I mounted the pulpit steps to find an ease in preaching, an almost wind-at-my-back type of situation.

A young man, weeping, approached me after the meeting. 'God has spoken to me tonight,' he said. 'I want to become a Christian.' He wept his way to the Saviour. The three men who had prayed with me before the service had no doubt about where the victory lay. Neither had I.

September 30

I was a stranger and ye took me in
MATTHEW 25:35

One stormy evening an elderly man and his wife asked for accommodation in a small Philadelphia hotel. The clerk told them that every guest room was taken but that since it was such a wild night he could not send them out into the rain. He gave them his own bedroom.

Two years passed and one day the clerk got a letter containing a round-trip ticket to New York. It was from the elderly gentleman who had occupied his bedroom on that stormy night. He asked the clerk to join him on his visit to New York.

The clerk went to New York and was led to the corner of Fifth Avenue and Thirty-fourth Street. There the old man showed him a vast new building of reddish stone called the Waldorf-Astoria, which was to become one of the most famous hotels in the world. 'That', declared the old man, 'is the hotel I have just built for you to manage.' George C. Boldt was glad he had given up his bedroom to the man who turned out to be William Waldorf Astor!

So be careful how you treat strangers.

October 1

A son honoureth his father, and a servant his master: if then I be a father, where is mine honour? and if I be a master, where is my fear?
MALACHI 1:6

The book of Malachi is a vivid encounter between God and his people. In Israel everybody knew that a son should honour his father and a servant his master. It was a shock therefore when, through Malachi, God turned and said to them: 'If I be a father, where is mine honour? And if I be a master, where is my fear?'

What is the point of you and I calling God 'Our Father' if we do not honour him. It is the sin of profanity. It is to take that which is sacred and make it merely commonplace.

How can we honour our father? We can set him highest in our thoughts, we can trust in his name, we can obey him, we can praise him, we can grieve when his name suffers and we can honour the Lord Jesus and thus obey the command: 'That all men should honour the Son, even as they honour the Father' (John 5:23).

'If I be a master, where is my fear?' This should be the true relationship between God and his people, that of the master/servant relationship. We love our master and we will not go out free. We do not 'Fear him' in the sense that we are frightened out of our wits of him. We fear God in that we reverence him above everything.

October 2

And if ye offer the blind for sacrifice, is it not evil? and if ye offer the lame and the sick, is it not evil? offer it now unto thy governor; will he be pleased with thee, or accept thy person? saith the Lord of Hosts
MALACHI 1:8

The complaint here is that of sacrilege in offering God something which costs nothing. It is misusing something sacred. The divine requirement was that the lamb should be without spot or blemish — the finest of the flock. These people retained the finest of the flock for themselves and

133

brought to the altar the blind, the lame and the sick. God is saying to Israel — 'Would you offer the Governor who rules over your city such a mean offering?' Why would people offer God what they would not offer an earthly ruler?

Remember God always values what we offer him not by its intrinsic worth but by what it cost us to bring it. The widow with her mites, the Saviour pointed out, cast in 'more than they all'.

October 3

Who is there even among you that would shut doors for nought? neither do ye kindle fire on mine altar for nought
MALACHI 1:10

These people obviously anticipated gain in doing God's work. Men opened doors and kindled fires to gain reward. Is our service for God's glory or for our own gain? Honestly ask yourself before God today: 'Would I do this action if I knew no one would ever find out, if my name were never to be linked with it and others were to get the credit for my hard work?'

Who is there among us who will render God service for very love of him? When will the sin of greed go out of our service? Let the question sink deep into your conscience today.

October 4

Ye said also, Behold, what a weariness is it! and ye have snuffed at it
MALACHI 1:13

In this twentieth century we hear the groan from Christendom that religion is a weariness. God a weariness to them! Look at their incense and vestments and weary traditions. Just recently at a meeting a lady told me she had been attending a certain church for years where the gospel

134

was not preached, where form and ceremony were to the fore and she had grown weary of the whole thing. I'm glad to say that she did not let that weariness with a Christless religion turn her from Christ. She then said, quietly, 'I received the Lord as Saviour tonight.' No longer weary I watched her walk off into the night rejoicing in sins forgiven and possessing peace with God.

October 5

Ye have wearied the Lord with your words. Yet ye say, Wherein have we wearied him? When ye say, Every one that doeth evil is good in the sight of the Lord, and he delighteth in them; or, Where is the God of judgement?
MALACHI 2:17

This was treason. This was excusing sin.

Have we not seen this problem in the church today? The people who are weary of a strong and robust Christianity and seek a glorified 'Saturday Night at the Proms' type of worship simply cannot bear to be told of the judgement of God.

Because God is a God of love we must remember that that love is the sworn enemy of sin. If God will excuse sin in us he will excuse our ruin. Judgement comes because of God's love. It is a false conception of love which says God is not a God of judgement.

Let us never excuse or cover up sin. Calvary's cross and the wrath of God which fell upon the Saviour, dying on our behalf, showed very clearly what God thought of sin.

October 6

Will a man rob God? Yet ye have robbed me. But ye say, Wherein have we robbed thee? In tithes and offerings
MALACHI 3:8

Robbery in heaven! The people had brought tithes to God, they had responded to his claim. Was this not enough? No. God demanded a tithe only as a minimum and they had robbed God in that they had not responded to God's claim

135

in the spirit in which it was made. They were not responding in the spirit of love. If your tithe is out of harmony with your success in life, it is wrong. Give God a tithe of your earnings for sure, but let that only be a minimum; respond in love over and above the tithe as he prospers you.

October 7

Your words have been stout against me, saith the Lord. Yet ye say, What have we spoken so much against thee? Ye have said, It is vain to serve God: and what profit is it that we have kept his ordinance, and that we have walked mournfully before the Lord of Hosts?
MALACHI 3:13, 14

This attitude is one to which God's servants are particularly prone when times are hard. Many who have served God for years but have allowed the devil to get them down become discouraged and say 'It is vain to serve God; and what profit is it that we have kept his ordinance?' It is on account of hypocritical living by believers that the Church of Christ on earth is doing little to lift the world to heaven and God.

As my friend Noel Grant put it: 'A drunkard and blasphemer is of far less use to the devil than a backslider.'

October 8

The burden of the word of the Lord to Israel by Malachi. I have loved you, saith the Lord
MALACHI 1:1, 2

As we have considered the depths to which God's people had reached in bringing down on themselves the anger of God against their sin, it is truly moving to read this overriding statement of God. God is saying:

'Despite all you have done — I have loved you!'

He fed them, he carried them (and their grumbling, disobedient forebearers) through all the days. He bore with them and waited patiently for them. In 'the years in which he was grieved with them' this burden of love was ever present.

The divine attitude to you is: 'I have loved you.'

What, then, is yours?

October 9

Then they that feared the Lord spake often one to another
MALACHI 3:16

God has never left himself without a definite and clear witness to his truth. There have been times in the world's history when it has seemed as though the whole world were given over to darkness: but it has never been so.

'I, even I, only am left,' said Elijah to God.

'I have left me seven thousand in Israel, all the knees which have not bowed unto Baal,' answered God.

So it was in Malachi's day. There was fearful spiritual darkness all over Israel; profanity, sacrilege, greed, blasphemy and weariness. Still, here was a group drawn together in fellowship because they feared the Lord. They were open to his guidance, will and authority, they wished to serve and obey him. They were the light in darkness.

Tell me, are you their twentieth century counterpart? Do you have fellowship with those of a like mind?

October 10

*A book of remembrance was written before him for them
that feared the Lord, and that thought upon his name*
MALACHI 3:16

It is the latter part of this verse that we want to think about today. Not only did these elect remnant of Malachi's day fear the Lord — they thought upon his name. They esteemed his name, they regarded his name, it was the chief thing. Their treasure was his name and where their treasure was their heart nestled. There can be no greater occupation than to think upon his name. It is a name far above all others.

His name is as ointment poured forth. Think of God in Christ as:

The Regenerator. The Rose of Sharon. The Rock.

The Reconciler. The Root of David. The Revealer.

The Redeemer. The Saviour. The Sufferer. The Star.

The Shepherd. The Servant. The Priest. The Prince.

The Son of God. The Prophet. The Preciousness.

The Potter. The Physician. The Purifier.

The Passover

October 11

The Call of God — *'Bring ye all the tithes into the storehouse'*

The Challenge of God — *'And prove me now herewith, saith the Lord of hosts'*

The Promise of God — *'If I will not open you the windows of heaven, and pour you out a blessing, that there shall not be room enough to receive it. And I will rebuke the devourer for your sakes, and he shall not destroy the fruits of your ground; neither shall your vine cast her fruit before the time in the field'*

The Result — *'And all nations shall call you blessed; for ye shall be a delightsome land, saith the Lord of hosts'*

MALACHI 3:10-12

October 12

I . . .

Suffer long
Am kind
Envy not
Vaunt not myself
Am not puffed up
Do not behave myself unseemly
Seek not my own
Am not easily provoked
Think no evil

138

Rejoice not in iniquity
Rejoice with the truth
Bear all things
Believe all things
Hope all things
Endure all things
1 CORINTHIANS 13:4-7

P.S. My name is love

October 13

Let us lay aside every weight ... and run the race with patience
HEBREWS 12:1

Have you to make a big decision in your life today? If you have, would you ask yourself these five questions, praying that the Holy Spirit will guide you in giving honest answers as you make your decision?
1. Will it be a wing or a weight?
2. Does it honour the Lord?
3. Will it make a weaker Christian stumble?
4. Can you pray about it with an untroubled mind?
5. Can you praise God for it?
Always remember what the housewife said when her husband asked her whether or not his shirt collar was dirty: 'If it's doubtful it's dirty!'

October 14

... Therefore Sarah laughed
GENESIS 18:12

For what will you be remembered? Very often just one incident in a person's life will stand out in the memory when a multitude of others have faded.

Think of Sarah. Unfortunately we can call to mind only too quickly the fact that Sarah laughed at the promises of God. It is true that the angels appeared to Abraham in the form of what seemed ordinary and very human men. It is true that Sarah was 'old and well stricken in age'. When Sarah heard the messengers inform her husband that she would have a son it may have *seemed* laughable. But God's promises are not to be laughed at, to be carelessly thrown aside as 'too impossible'. Those who treat God's promises in this way suffer great loss.

October 15

Hath not God made foolish the wisdom of this world?
1 CORINTHIANS 1:20

> See that there young preacher?
> He's fresh out of school,
> He don't know my Jesus,
> He's an educated fool.

Sung by Mahalia Jackson

October 16

What is man . . .?
PSALM 8:4

Someone once wrote a very good description of man:
> Crumbled desires
> Crushed pride
> Bruised heart
> Salvage for God.

Yes, God can take you and all your broken pieces and make of you a new creature in Christ Jesus. You are more than just a chemical mass, you have a soul that can be regenerated by the power of the gospel of Jesus Christ if you will but believe. No life that will ever read these lines is beyond the reach of regenerating power of the Lord Jesus. Salvage? God can salvage the wreck of your life this very moment. Rethink your position, renounce your past life, repent of your sins, and receive the Lord Jesus as your Saviour: *now*.

140

October 17

Is not the arrow beyond thee?
1 SAMUEL 20:37

Jonathan came down to keep his pact with David. The pact was that if he shouted to the little lad with him that the arrow he had shot was 'beyond thee', the hidden David was to take this as the signal that King Saul was intent on killing him. If Jonathan were to cry: 'The arrows are on this side of thee', then David was to understand that all was well and that he could safely come out of hiding.

Can you imagine how David felt that day as he watched Jonathan walk towards his hiding place by the stone Ezel? Would it be reconciliation with Saul? No, he could hear Jonathan shouting, 'Is not the arrow beyond thee?' It meant the road of a fugitive and outcast for him.

Perhaps, like David, you are out of favour at the moment through no fault of your own. Perhaps you have chosen God's way and you have lost your social standing and reputation in the eyes of men. If the arrow is beyond today then get up and go on in the knowledge that there is a divine purpose determining your course and that the going forth is necessary to secure greater happiness than you leave. Follow the arrow's light from the known out into the unknown. Be like Abraham and head for the land which God will show you: this is the way to the throne.

October 18

And he led them forth by the right way, that they might go to a city of habitation
PSALM 107:7

HE led! Who led? None other than the Almighty God.

He LED! This was no God far removed from the needs of his people. He went out before them and led them.

He led THEM! Who? A grumbling, complaining, weary, troubled, distressed people.

141

He led . . . by a WAY! This was a wilderness, there was no road to be seen! But God saw a way through and beyond.

He led them a STRAIGHT way! Not straight in the sense of a straight line but a straight way under the conditions of travel at that time.

He led them that they might GO! If you settle down you cannot be led. Contentment with this world and satisfaction with the present precludes guidance.

He led them . . . to A CITY! God is leading to a city of permanent safety and peace, to a kingdom which cannot be shaken.

. . . a city of HABITATION! The wanderings of the wilderness are past: the city of God has been gained. We shall go there to dwell in that city and go out no more.

October 19

A false balance is abomination to the Lord: but a just weight is his delight
PROVERBS 11:1

You've heard the one about the pompous tax inspector, I'm sure. He called on a farmer to check his wage records.

'How many employees do you have?'

'Two,' said the elderly farmer.

'What do you pay them?'

'What the usual agricultural rate is, plus overtime.'

'No other staff?'

'No other staff . . . except the half-wit.'

And what does he get?'

'A pound a week, his meals and a pair of trousers every Christmas.'

'H'm,' said the inspector, after making a note. 'I'd like to see him.'

'See him?' snapped the exasperated farmer. 'You're talking to him!'

142

October 20

G. H. Lang writes of an experience he had in 1935. He says, 'I was travelling by rail from Haifa to Cairo. As I neared Cairo I remembered that an Egyptian child of mine in faith, converted perhaps twenty years before, had been sent in government service to Aswan, the southernmost town in Egypt, perhaps 500 miles from Cairo. It came upon my heart that, in spite of the long journey, I must visit him and see as to his spiritual welfare. On reaching Cairo I found a letter from his wife. It had been sent to England, and had been returned, reaching Cairo the very day I did, and it said that, should the Lord again send me to Egypt, they hoped I would visit them, and the money for the journey was enclosed. One interesting item was that the writer, an American, had married my friend some two years before, yet had only now written to introduce herself to me.'

Do you know anything about such experiences? Have you asked the Lord to guide you in recent times or have you got to such a position that you do all the arranging and God is ignored? What a dull, useless, empty, godless life you must be leading! How very unexciting!

October 21

There are only four kinds of children. There is 'the child that never was', the child who is the dream of all lonely men and women who have never known marriage and the delights of a home of their own.

There is 'the child that was', a gladsome gift that death snatched away. 'The child that was' never grows up, it either drives its parents to bitterness or deeper service for the Shepherd who took their lamb across the river first.

'The child that is' is best known. He is all around us and is a mixture of curiosity, ambition and imagination. One

143

of the greatest gifts we parents can give to 'the child that is' is our time. I love the story of Joseph Lister, the eminent surgeon. Coming out of the operating theatre where he had just performed a major operation, he met a little girl, a patient in the hospital, who asked him to operate on her doll. He skilfully gave of his time and sewed up the doll so that the stuffing wouldn't come out.

The fourth child is 'the child that is yet to be'. If you, reader, are a young man can I ask you a very personal question? When the girl of your choice is in your arms are you securing for 'the child that is yet to be' a mother who will uphold the great traditions of motherhood and one who knows and loves the Saviour? If you, reader, are a young lady has that lover of yours footsteps into which you long that 'the child that is yet to be' will put his?

October 22

Be not as the hypocrites, of a sad countenance
MATTHEW 6:16

A smile costs nothing, but gives much. It enriches those who receive, without making poorer those who give. It takes but a moment, yet the memory of it might last forever. A smile creates happiness in the home, fosters goodwill in business, and is the sign of friendship. It brings rest to the weary, cheer to the discouraged, sunshine to the sad, and is nature's best antidote to trouble.

Yet a smile cannot be bought, begged, borrowed or stolen; for it is something of no value to anyone unless it is given away.

October 23

Better is the end of a thing than the beginning thereof
ECCLESIASTES 7:8

Will not the end explain
The crossed endeavour, earnest purpose foiled.
The strange bewilderment of good walk spoiled,
The clinging weariness, the inward strain,
Will not the end explain?

Meanwhile he comforteth
Them that are losing patience. 'Tis his way:
But none can write the words they hear him say
For men to read: only they know he saith
Sweet words, and comforteth.

Not that he doth explain
The mystery that baffleth; but a sense
Husheth the quiet heart, that far, far hence
Lieth a field set thick with golden grain
Wetted in seeding days by many a rain:
The end — it will explain.

Amy Carmichael

October 24

. . . If the whole were hearing, where were the smelling?
1 CORINTHIANS 12:17

Maybe a Christian reader is feeling despised because of the seemingly insignificant role you have been given by the Lord. Could I quote to you a beautiful piece of writing which means a lot to me? I don't know who wrote it, but here it is:

'I was tired and sat down under the shadow of the great pines in a Swedish forest, glad to find such a cool retreat from the broiling sun. I had not been there long before I noticed a fragrant odour and wondered what it could be and from where it came. No Marchiel Niel rose grew on that barren soil, nor could the sun penetrate the shades of the forest to extract its perfume even if it had; I looked around, and found by my side a tiny flower about half the size of an ordinary daisy, nearly hidden from view by the moss. It was the little "Linea blomma!"
I thought, why is it so obscure, when it is a flower with such fragrance, and surely worthy a place in the most stately grounds? I learned a lesson by it and it spoke to my heart. I thought, if I cannot be a pine in God's forest, I may be a tiny flower to send forth the fragrance of Jesus in this world of sadness.'

October 25

Let your light so shine before men
MATTHEW 5:16

Lighthouses don't fire guns or ring bells to call attention to their light, they just shine.

October 26

And Zacchaeus stood, and said . . . Lord . . . if I have taken any thing from any man by false accusation, I restore him fourfold
LUKE 19:8

Festo Kivengere tells the story that his uncle, the Chief, was sitting in court one day with his courtiers around him when a man came and bowed in the African way. He was rich in cattle and was well known as a man who sought God through the spirit of dead relatives. He had come with eight cows which he left some twenty yards away.

'I have come for a purpose, Sir,' the man said.

'What are those cows for?' asked the Chief.

'Sir, they are yours.'

'What do you mean, they are mine?'

'They are yours. When I was looking after your cattle, I stole four and now they are eight, and I bring them to you.'

'Who arrested you?'

'Jesus arrested me, Sir, and here are your cows.'

There was no laughter, only shocked silence. My uncle could see this man was at peace with himself and rejoicing.

'You can put me in prison or beat me up,' the man said, 'but I am liberated. Jesus came my way and I am a free human being.'

'Well, if God has done this for you, who am I to put you in prison? You go home.'

A few days later, having heard the news, Festo went to see his uncle. He said to him, 'Uncle, I hear you got eight free cows!'

'Yes, it's true,' his uncle replied.

'You must be happy.'

'Forget it! Since that man came, I can't sleep. If I want the peace he has, I would have to return a hundred cows.'

146

October 27

Rejoice, because your names are written in heaven
LUKE 10:20

The security of heaven is   — his power.
The light of heaven is   — his face.
The joy of heaven is   — his presence.
The melody of heaven is   — his name.
The harmony of heaven is   — his praise.
The theme of heaven is   — his work.
The employment of heaven is   — his service.
The duration of heaven is   — his eternity.
The only man-made thing in heaven is the print of the
    nails in his hands.
Is your name written there?

October 28

*And David said to Abigail, Blessed be the Lord god of Israel,
which sent thee this day to meet me: And blessed be thy
advice*
1 SAMUEL 25:32, 33

*Michal . . . saw king David . . . dancing before the Lord . . .
and she despised him in her heart*
2 SAMUEL 6:16

Be warned, whoever you are and whatever situation you are
in, there are Abigails in this world and there are Michals. The
Abigails bring warmth, love, affection, blessing and
edification wherever they go. They warn God's men when
they are in danger, they dissuade them from actions which
would bring dishonour on the Lord's name and the results of
their practical action is inestimable.

The Michals of this world are cold, critical, power
seeking, selfish and downright carnal. The Michals begin by
loving their husbands and end by despising them. The cares
of other things, the deceitfulness of riches enter in and
choke their love and any spirituality there is.

An Abigail will make a man and a Michal will break
him.

October 29

Let me be weighed in an even balance
JOB 31:6

Aim to be:
Conciliatory — but not servile.
Winning — but not fawning.
Timely — but not time-serving.
Simple — but not commonplace.
Interesting — but not sensational.
Direct — but not blunt.
Positive — but not dogmatic.
Bold — but not boisterous.
Tender — but not sentimental.
Orderly — but not mechanical.
Balanced, yes balanced, is the word!

October 30

*And the things that thou has heard of me ... the same
commit ... to faithful men, who shall be able to teach others*
2 TIMOTHY 2:2

Perhaps I will be accused of mere sentimentality but
thousands in our land remember an older generation who
faithfully took time to teach us the word of God. Some of
them may be encouraged by these lines written by a young
man about his old Sunday School teacher.

'The Noisy Seven'

I wonder if he remembers
That dear old man in heaven
The class in the old red schoolhouse,
Known as 'The Noisy Seven'.
I wonder if he remembers
How useless we used to be,
Or thinks we forgot the lessons
Of Christ and Gethsemane?
I wish I could tell that story,
As he used to tell it then,
I think that with heaven's blessing,
I could reach the hearts of men.

I often wish I could tell him,
Though we caused him so much pain
By our thoughtless boyish frolics,
His lessons were not in vain.
I'd like to tell him how Harry,
The noisiest one of all,
From the mission fields of Shiloh,
Went home at the Master's call.
I'd like to tell him how Stephen,
So brimming with life and fun,
Now tells to the people of Asia,
The tale of the crucified one.

I'd like to tell how Joseph,
And Philip and Jack and Ray,
Are honoured among God's workers,
The foremost men of their day.
I'd like, yes, I'd like to tell him,
What his lessons did for me,
And how I'm trying to follow
The Christ of Gethsemane.
Perhaps he knows already,
For Harry has told maybe,
That we are all coming — coming,
Through Christ and Gethsemane.

How many besides, I know not,
Will gather at last in heaven,
The fruits of that faithful sowing,
But the sheaves are surely seven.

October 31

For we walk by faith not by sight
2 CORINTHIANS 5:7

One day, as I walked along, I heard a voice call me.
Whoever he was he knew my name and he said: 'This is the
way, walk ye in it.' What way? 'I am the way,' said the voice.
Stumbling, frightened and seeing nobody I got down on my
knees. I saw I was on the edge of not only darkness but
eternal darkness, and hearing the voice calling again, I
followed. Soon I found the person who called me and

admitting I had been on the wrong path I accepted him as my guide and trusting him there and then, he led me on. I have not got to the end of the pathway yet. But I am assured by him that what he has begun he will complete. Even though I walk through the valley of mists, I will fear no evil. I still encounter plenty but then I've got him now and he knows the way through the mists: all I have to do is to follow.

November 1

He that hath the Son hath life
1 JOHN 5:12

There once lived a very rich man. His house was so beautiful that everybody simply referred to it as 'The House'. People either came to 'The House' or walked by 'The House', or were instructed to look out for 'The House'. It contained the most beautiful collection of paintings in the country.

This rich man had only one son, and he loved him very much. Imagine the shock when his son died. It broke his heart, and because he missed his son so much the father himself lost the will to live. After his death there was an auction of the famous paintings at 'The House'. All sorts of rich people attended the auction and most of them wanted to buy one painting at least out of the famous collection. The auctioneer stood up to begin the auction.

'Now today, ladies and gentlemen,' he said, 'the first painting to be put up for sale is a portrait of the boy who used to live in this house. How much am I bid?'

There was silence. The people present thought that the painting was not worth buying because it had not been painted by a famous painter. But there was one person who did not consider the painting worthless. He was the gardener. He had known the rich man's son very well and thought the world of him. He could not bear to see the memory of the lad despised, so, despite the fact that he felt embarrassed amongst such a well-dressed and distinguished crowd, he spoke up. 'I bid, sir,' he said. He got the painting for a few pounds, and was just turning away when he heard the auctioneer say, 'This auction is now over.'

'Over?' enquired the crowd. 'How can it be over when all the great paintings have yet to be sold?'

'The paintings are not going to be sold,' replied the auctioneer.

'And why not?' asked the now astonished crowd.

'Simply because the owner of this house left a will that whoever bought the painting of his son would get all the rest of these beautiful paintings and the house as well for nothing,' replied the auctioneer quietly.

There is another Son, whom many treat as worthless. He is the Son of God. One man actually sold him to a crowd of religious hypocrites to be crucified, for thirty pieces of silver. That's all the price he put upon the Christ of God.

Yet, there are a few who wisely see his true worth and count his love to be beyond measure or price. They would rather, in life, be lead by his nail-pierced hand. They believe the scripture when it says: 'He that *hath the Son*, hath life.' They are the wise ones, for theirs are spiritual and eternal riches beyond measure, for 'as many as received him to them gave he power to become the Sons of God, even to them that believe on his name.'

November 2

Jehovah — jireh   The Lord will provide
GENESIS 22:13, 14

Jehovah — rapha   The Lord that healeth
EXODUS 15:26

Jehovah — shalom   The Lord our peace
JUDGES 6:23, 24

Jehovah — tsidkenu   The Lord our righteousness
JEREMIAH 23:6

Jehovah — nissi   The Lord our banner
EXODUS 17:8-15

Jehovah — ra-ah   The Lord my shepherd
Psalm 23:1

Jehovah — shammah   The Lord ever-present
EZEKIEL 48:35

November 3

Cleanse thou me from secret faults
PSALM 19:12

Do you find it hard to make friends? Maybe you need first to get properly clean before God. If you are holding on to fear, guilt, anger or worry you will give impressions of fear, guilt, anger and worry to others who meet you. The Christian must be as transparent as a mountain stream. You must have a clean heart and God has given you his promise and power to be free. If you have been hurt, forgive. If you have things to put right, do so. You must be clean: this is the first step to making friends.

November 4

Honour thy father and thy mother: that thy days may be long upon the land which the Lord thy God giveth thee
EXODUS 20:12

How can you honour parents if they are alcoholics, or atheists, or sadistic, or divorced, or careless, or of different faiths?

You must honour the fact that they are your father and mother no matter how big a mess their lives might be in. After all your life was a mess when the Lord Jesus entered in and cleansed it. Live quietly before them, less by lip than by life. If they rebel, love them all the more, for Jesus' sake and for their own. No matter how hurt you may feel by their faults, look beyond their faults and see their need. God will honour you beyond anything you could ever ask or think.

November 5

I looked on my right hand, and beheld, but there was no man that would know me: refuge failed me; no man cared for my soul
PSALM 142:4

These words of David run deep. Anointed of God for the throne of Israel, hero of Goliath's defeat, subject of the song of Israel's maidens, master of sword and harp and yet the very same David says, 'No man cared for my soul'.

It is a cry many a man of God could echo. People are often greatly caring for the souls of the ungodly but care not for the nurture and encouragement of the souls of the converted. Enough for them that the sheep are in the fold, they care not if they starve of hunger. Many a young person is longing for a word of counsel, for a word of spiritual guidance, for food for their souls from you.

November 6

And David said in his heart, I shall now perish one day by the hand of Saul: there is nothing better for me than I should speedily escape into the land of the Philistines.
1 SAMUEL 27:1

Look where panic in David's heart took him when he let it. It took him right into the hands of the enemy, the very enemy who had run for miles for fear of him when he slew their champion Goliath with a single stone and faith in God.

His escape to the Philistines led to disaster, to lies, to cruelty and endless trouble. This is a warning: do not run into the arms of the enemy to escape the pressure of being a follower of the Lord Jesus Christ. Had not God made his promise to put David on the throne of Israel? Was God going to recant? *Never.* Has not God made promises to you that the good work he has begun he will complete, promising never to leave you nor forsake you? Wait for him. Escape into his promises not into the enemy's camp.

November 7

Man shall not live by bread alone, but by every word that proceedeth out of the mouth of God
MATTHEW 4:4

The Bible is a book that gives the answers to the deepest needs of the human heart; God's answers. Is there any human situation which you will not find mentioned there? Take the word of God today and find out what it has to say about *your* problem. It is all there for you to draw from and feed on. Leave the world's literature aside for a while today, fold up the newspaper, read the word. Take the advice of God to his people in Deuteronomy 6:7 and hide his word in your heart: 'When you sit in the house . . . when you walk in the way (bus, plane, train!) . . . when you lie down . . . when you rise up.'

November 8

Except the Lord build the house,
They labour in vain that build it.
Except the Lord keep the city,
The watchman waketh but in vain.
It is vain for you to rise up early,
To sit up late,
To eat the bread of sorrows:
For so he giveth his beloved sleep.
Lo, children are an heritage of the Lord.
And the fruit of the womb is his reward.
As arrows are in the hand of a mighty man;
So are children of the youth.
Happy is the man that hath his quiver full
   of them.
They shall not be ashamed, but they shall
Speak with the enemies in the gate.

PSALM 127

November 9

In quietness and in confidence shall be your strength
ISAIAH 30:15

Slow me down, Lord. Ease the pounding of my heart
      by the quieting of my mind.
Steady my unhurried pace with a vision of the eternal
      reach of time.
Give me, amid the confusion of the day, the calmness
      of the everlasting hills.
Break the tensions of my nerves and muscles with the
      soothing music of the singing streams that live
      in my memory.

Help me to know the magical, restoring power of
    sleep.
Teach me the art of taking minute vacations — of
    slowing down to look at a flower, to pat a dog,
    to read a few lines of a good book.
Slow me down, Lord, and inspire me to send my roots
    deep into the soul of life's unending values
    that I may grow toward the stars of my greater
    destiny.

Author unknown

November 10

This do in remembrance of me . . .
LUKE 22:19

Nice number out this morning. Ah! there's Tom, haven't
seen him for a long time, backsliding a bit recently, they say.
    Oh! There's Mary with a new outfit, bit trendy, doesn't
suit her.
    'Alas and did my Saviour bleed,
    And did my Sovereign die . . .'
    Singing is pretty dead this morning. Time we had a
new 'song leader'.
    'Would he devote that sacred head . . .'
    An awful draught from that window. They never get it
right in this place! They either have it like a hothouse or an
artic igloo.
    'For such a worm as I.'
    Isaiah 53 this morning? Pity he always reads it so fast,
far too hurried, slow down, man!
    'Despised and rejected of men . . .'
    Wonder who that row of strangers are? Don't fancy
the look of him!
    'He was led as a lamb to the slaughter
    and as a sheep before . . .'
    Wonder how tomorrow will go? Must ring Brian, early,
before he goes out to work.
    'He was numbered with the transgressors,
    and he bare the sin of many and made
    intercession for the transgressors.'

155

Not *another* speaker this morning! I've got to be at McKinnon's for lunch, early, they've got one of my old schoolmates coming, haven't seen him for years.

'Now finally, friends . . .'

You've said that three times already, sir! Finished? Amen! Announcements! If only he would read them and not rehash them.

'Good morning Mrs. Brown. Lovely meeting! Ah, Richard . . . I was just thinking during the meeting . . .'

November 11

They compel one Simon a Cyrenian, who passed by, coming out of the country, the father of Alexander and Rufus, to bear his cross
MARK 15:21

It was a seemingly 'chance' meeting. If Simon had entered the city one hour earlier his life story would have been entirely different. Yet, things were so ordered that he arrived at the right place, at exactly the right moment, and as on small hinges great doors are suspended, on small events tremendous issues may depend. Simon was enabled to bear Christ's cross.

I know not if Simon became a Christian; I know not what business caused him to travel from North Africa to Jerusalem: all I know is that his name will be forever remembered because he was associated with the cross of Christ. He did not know, as he hauled that cross up through the streets of Jerusalem that hot, crowd-throbbing day, that it was his finest hour.

November 12

Feed my sheep
JOHN 21:16

Willie Mullan, a converted tramp who as a young man was saved by God's grace when fast caught in a web of crime, lives in Lurgan, in the County of Armagh, Northern Ireland.

After his conversion he worked as chauffeur-cum-gardener for a surgeon in Newtonards, and sometimes he would drive his employer down to Stangford Lough to sail his yacht. As he waited for the surgeon's return Willie studied the Scriptures. It was indicative of his future life because when he eventually gave all his days to the preaching of God's word his gift for Bible teaching became the basis for what was without question the most unique Bible class in Europe.

For many years and for one and a half hours every Tuesday evening Willie taught hundreds of people the pure and powerful Scriptures. To have heard him teach has been one of my life's great experiences. It was in his class that I was called by God to preach the word.

His secret is unquestionably the hours he spends alone with the Lord Jesus in preparation. One day a pastor told him that he spent his time 'putting up chicken runs for old ladies' and helping out socially amongst God's people, and he accused Willie of not being involved enough, socially.

'How many do you preach to on the Lord's Day?' asked Willie.

'A few dozen,' bemoaned the pastor.

'Well, you go on putting up chicken runs for old ladies if you want and I'll spend my hours with the Book. I have 600 people to feed every Lord's Day,' replied the great Bible teacher.

November 13

Now then we are ambassadors for Christ
2 CORINTHIANS 5:20

We are the only Bibles
This careless world will read.
We are the sinners' gospel;
We are the scoffers' creed.
We are the Lord's last message,
Given in deed and word.
What if the type is crooked?
What if the print is blurred?

November 14

And a time to hate
ECCLESIASTES 3:8

The story is told of a godly Brighton man who bit his lips until they bled when he passed a man on the street whom he knew to be leading a good girl to her destruction. If our loves are wisely directed our hates will do nothing but good. If you love your flower beds you will hate weeds.

'Give me a hundred men who fear nothing but God, who hate nothing but sin, and who know nothing but Jesus Christ and him crucified and I will shake the world,' said John Wesley.

There is a time to hate. By a man's hates as well as his fruits, shall you know him.

November 15

He giveth power to the faint: and to them that have no might he increaseth strength
ISAIAH 40:29

They say that all power corrupts and that absolute power corrupts absolutely. In the world of human affairs that may be true but it is not true in the spiritual world. When God gives his power it never corrupts. This is because it is only given to the humble, who will invariably give God the glory. Spiritual power is given to the weak to confound the mighty.

It is hunger which gives food its taste. It is thirst which makes cool clear water taste like nectar. It is tiredness which makes sleep a boon. It is toil which makes rest the thing which the body and mind long for. It is loneliness which gives friendship its value. It is rain which gives the sunshine its joy. It is the dark of the night which gives the dawn its glory. It is parting which makes reuniting a happy thing.

It is just a weak, failing and fragile Christian like you whom God would delight to demonstrate his power through if you were willing to obey him and give him the glory. Weakness is no excuse, man, it is a qualification!

November 16

Humble thyself, and make sure thy friend
PROVERBS 6:3

I used to have an English teacher called Mr. Watts. He taught me many things but one gem I shall not forget. He was training me to speak at an inter-schools' Debating Competition and I had to speak my written speech before him at lunch-time.

I went up to his room and there he was reading his newspaper and taking his soup and sandwiches at his desk. I stood at the back of the room and began my speech. Before long I made a mistake and began to get annoyed with myself.

'Bingham,' he said, looking over his famous half-rimmed glasses, 'if you ever make a mistake in a speech in public, never be afraid to *laugh at yourself*!'

November 17

My peace I give unto you: not as the world giveth, give I unto you
JOHN 14:27

How does the world give? It gives pleasure for a season. It gives wreaths that wither. It gives money that buys cars, beautiful homes, jewellery, perfumes, literature, real estate, jet travel, education, medicine, food and a million other things. Yet never will that money in a million years buy one single moment of real deep down peace.

The Saviour, on the other hand, gives peace which will never be taken away from its possessor. Not as the world gives at all. Not a false hope, not a false joy, not a thrill-for-the-moment. He gives eternal peace that all hell cannot shake or disturb. Do you know this peace? Then enjoy it and flirt no more with the world. Do you not possess it? Then receive the Lord Jesus as your Saviour now.

159

November 18

They took the thirty pieces of silver, the price of him that was valued
MATTHEW 27:9

'There is something utterly nauseating about a system of society which pays a harlot 25 times as much as it pays its Prime Minister, 250 times as much as it pays its Members of Parliament, and 500 times as much as it pays some of its ministers of religion.'

Sir Harold Wilson

(On the case of Christine Keeler. Speech in House of Commons, 1963.)

November 19

So likewise ye, when ye shall have done all those things which are commanded you, We are unprofitable servants: we have done that which was our duty to do
LUKE 17:10

To follow a clear sense of duty is always safe. I once made a promise, which in a turn of events I could have quite legitimately got out of. If I stayed by it I would have to lose financially, if I went back on it others would be hurt. I was caught between two ways.

There was only one way; I knew I must stay by my promise, come what may. Others thought I was mad but I knew God would not fail me. Did He? Of course not, the financial need was met; the promise kept and my heart was at peace. To follow a clear sense of duty is *always* safe. Do not let apparent risks which rise when the call to duty is clear ever at any time disturb your peace about doing your duty.

November 20

And in all things, whatsoever ye shall ask in prayer, believing ye shall receive
MATTHEW 21:22

By May 26th 1850, there were, we are told, in George Muller's Orphanage at Bristol, 275 orphan children. Scarcely were they housed on Ashley Down before George

160

Muller's heart felt a desire that 1,000 children might be housed! He prayed about it in faith. God answered his prayer, sent him tens of thousands of pounds and by 1870 there were five large buildings on Ashley Down — accommodating 1,000 orphans? No, not at all. Just 2,000 orphans!

No longer be content with the daily round, for, 'Out there beyond the horizon, there's more, there's more.'

November 21

Now therefore, our God, we thank thee, and praise thy glorious name
1 CHRONICLES 29:13

To forget to be thankful leads to arrogant self-sufficiency and to doubting God when that self-sufficiency is tested and found to be useless. A dull memory is the ally of ingratitude. A redeemed memory, closely allied with truth, does not allow ingratitude to rise, it keenly remembers the 'rock from which it was hewn' and this is disastrous to pride and all its cohorts.

November 22

Let not thy left hand know what thy right hand doeth
MATTHEW 6:3

What does it matter who gets the credit so long as the work is done? Humble yourself under the mighty hand of God. Cover your tracks when you set out into the forest to do some good deed! Efface self and enjoy doing it, don't endure it. Go on a grand binge of doing a string of good deeds this week deliberately seeking to keep Christ to the fore and self nailed to his cross. Tell no one but him and see what kind of a week you have. You will find it to have been one of the most spiritually healthy weeks you have ever known.

November 23

Fret not
PSALM 37:1

Are you bitter today? Are you in an angry, frustrated, rebellious, ready-to-throw-in-the-towel attitude? Then if you say that you believe God is there and loves you and then live through today as if he were dead or couldn't care less about you, you are in fact practising a pathetic view of God which would do no credit to a pagan.

Faith is better tested in a crisis than in a creed.

November 24

Ask, and it shall be given you
MATTHEW 7:7

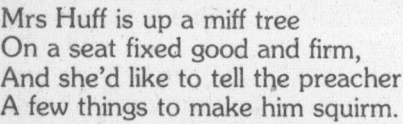

Mrs Huff is up a miff tree
On a seat fixed good and firm,
And she'd like to tell the preacher
A few things to make him squirm.

Mrs Huff was sick abed, sir,
Yes, sir, sick abed a week;
And the preacher didn't call, sir,
Not even took a peek.

Wasn't that enough, enough, sir
To provoke a saint to wrath?
And to make a Christian pilgrim
Wander from the churchly path?

When I asked if the doctor
Called to see her, she said, 'Sure'
And she looked as if she thought I
Needed some good strong mind cure.

Then I asked her how the doctor knew
That sickness laid her low,
And she said that she had called him
On the phone and told him so.

So the doctor called to see her,
But the preacher didn't go,
For the doctor knew that she was ill
And the preacher didn't know.

Now the doctor gets his bill paid
With a nicely written cheque,
But the preacher — for not knowing,
Simply 'gets it in the neck'.

W. C. Summers

November 25

The house was filled with the odour of the ointment
JOHN 12:3

No one could come into his presence without smelling the fragrant odours of love, compassion and tenderness. The wickedness of the human heart, which he met on every hand, only disclosed his preciousness more and more. Let us then not be despondent over what we are and what we are not. Let our attention be more than ever directed to him, so that when he fills our vision everything else may vanish. As his sweetness fills the soul, so will his fragrance flow forth from us as the outcome of communion with him.

November 26

There shall be no loss . . .
ACTS 27:22

To talk with God
No breath is lost
— Talk on!

To walk with God
No strength is lost
— Walk on!

To wait on God
No time is lost
— Wait on!

163

November 27

Covetousness, which is idolatry
COLOSSIANS 3:5

Covetousness is a miserable beggar: it draws away from the God who satisfies, to false gods who pollute the fountain head of blessing.

Coveting a Babylonish garment led Achan to become a thief.

Coveting money led Judas to treason.

Coveting a piece of ground, a vineyard, led King Ahab to murder.

Coveting the world rather than the service of Christ in company of the Apostle Paul led Demas to apostasy.

Reader, for all your life, and for the sake of your soul, be content with such things as you have.

November 28

That which cometh upon me daily, the care of all the churches
2 CORINTHIANS 11:28

When I see the modern day apostasy of many in Christendom, the denying of the virgin birth, the denying of the inspiration of Scripture, the hatred of plain gospel preaching I feel like Samuel Rutherford when he wrote to Lady Boyd in 1637 after he had been 'exiled' to Aberdeen for his faithfulness to God's word:

> 'This apostate kirk hath played the harlot with many lovers; they are spitting in the face of my lovely King, and mocking him, and I cannot mend it; and they are running away from Christ in troops, and I cannot mourn and be grieved for it. I think Christ lieth like an old unused castle, forsaken of the inhabitants: all men run away now from him . . .
>
> ' . . . Madame, pity me in this, and help me to praise him: for whatever I be, the chief of sinners, a devil, and a most guilty devil, yet it is the apple of Christ's eye, his honour and glory as Head of the Church, that I suffer for now, and that I go to eternity with.'

Have we such men today? Yes, I have met some who would lay down their life for love to Christ and his people. But they are few, mighty few.

November 29

And God saw that the wickedness of man was great in the earth, and that the imagination of the thoughts of his heart was only evil continually ... but Noah found grace in the sight of the Lord
GENESIS 6:5-8

You cannot choose your ancestry,
But you can choose your destiny.

November 30

When ye pray, use not vain repetitions, as the heathen do
MATTHEW 6:7

Have you heard someone pray like this: 'Oh, Father, I thank you, Father, that you, Father, can hear, Father ...'? Such people are only using words to fill in space and such is vain repetition. I once heard a preacher say, 'Dear friend in the meeting tonight' 81 times in the course of 35 minutes. I know because I counted them! Prayer is the most powerful ministry any believer can engage in and it is good to have a reputation in hell for being a prayerful Christian. Let us be reverent and earnest in prayer for it is not a song nor is it a chant. Above everything else let us avoid vain repetition.

Satan laughs at the words we say
Smiles at our efforts from day to day.
But Satan trembles when he sees
The weakest saint upon his knees.

December 1

Let us search and try our ways, and turn again to the Lord
LAMENTATIONS 3:40

Fred Somebody, Tom Everybody, Peter Anybody and Joe Nobody were neighbours, but they were not like you and me — they were odd people and most difficult to understand.

All four belonged to the same church, but you would not have enjoyed fellowship with then. Everyone went fishing on the Lord's day, or stayed at home to watch television. Anybody could have gone regularly but was afraid Somebody wouldn't speak to him, so guess who went along — Nobody!

Nobody was the only decent one of the four. Nobody did the visitation. Nobody welcomed strangers at the door. Once they needed a Sunday School teacher. Everybody thought Anybody would do it, and Anybody thought Somebody would do it, and can you guess who did it? That's right — Nobody!

It happened that a fifth neighbour moved into the area who was not a Christian. Everybody thought Somebody should try to win him for Christ. Anybody could have made the effort. You probably know who finally won him: Nobody!

The moral of the story is that Everybody should try to help Somebody or Nobody will be a blessing to Anybody.

December 2

Christ in you, the hope of glory
COLOSSIANS 1:27

Not merely in the words you say,
Not only in your deeds confessed,
But in the most unconscious way,
Is Christ expressed.

Is it a beautific smile?
A holy light upon your brow?
Oh, no, I felt his Presence
When you laughed just now.

For me, 'twas not the truth you told,
To you so clear, to me still dim,
But when you came to me, you brought
A glimpse of him.

And from your eyes he beckons me,
And from your lips his love is shed,
Till I lose sight of you, and see,
The Christ instead.

Anon.

December 3

Pleasant words are as an honeycomb, sweet to the soul, and health to the bones
PROVERBS 16:24

Sometimes I listen to people talk, particularly clever people who try to analyse things to such a pitch that the simple beauties and joys of life become very complicated. For example they say:

Scintillate, scintillate, globule vivific,
How I consider thy nature specific,
Loftily poised in the ether capacious,
Strongly resembling a gem carbonaceous.

You and I, simple down to earth folk would render it:

Twinkle, twinkle, little star,
How I wonder what you are,
Up above the clouds so high,
Like a diamond in the sky.

Let us call a spade, a spade, not an agricultural implement; a stormy night, a stormy night, not 'inclement weather'.

When we communicate the greatest message on earth, the gospel message, let us tell it as our Saviour told it, in a plain, straightforward, homely, interesting fashion. Is it any wonder they 'heard him gladly'? Let's be done with the tired, boring phrases of men and by using the brains God has given us choose fresh, down-to-earth language and let us pick our words with care, never being afraid to pour thick maple syrup on our hot cakes so that people will be more inclined to eat them.

December 4

And the clouds drop down the dew
PROVERBS 3:20

'Have you no clouds?' they asked an old saint.

'Sure!' he replied. 'Where else would my showers of blessings come from?'

December 5

Seekest thou great things for thyself? seek them not
JEREMIAH 45:5

I never read of C. H. Spurgeon without being moved by the story of the day he headed over Midsummer Common to the little wooden bridge which leads to Chesterton. He was about eighteen at the time and by a rare set of circumstances he had just missed an opportunity for higher education.

'In the midst of the Common', he recalls, 'I was startled by what seemed a loud voice . . . I seemed very distinctly to hear the words "Seekest thou great things for thyself? Seek them not" . . . I remembered the poor but loving people to whom I ministered, and the souls which had been given me in my humble charge; and although at that time I anticipated obscurity and poverty as the result of the resolve, yet I did there and then solemnly renounce the offer of Collegiate instruction, determining to abide for a season at least with my people, and to remain preaching the word so long as I had strength to do it. Had it not been for those words, in all probability I had never been where and what I now am.'

December 6

Withdraw thy foot from thy neighbour's house; lest he be weary of thee, and so hate thee
PROVERBS 25:17

One May evening I went to hear David Kossof, story-teller to the nation. I was intrigued with his white hair, little white Colonel Saunder's beard and his absolutely incredible gift

168

for telling stories, particularly Bible stories. Without a break he told stories for an hour and a half. It seemed but five minutes. How we all wished he had gone on much, much longer!

On his way off the platform Kossof stopped and said:

'My father was a poor Russian villager, simple in his way. He remained so until the day he died a poor tailor in London.

'One day my father took me aside,' he continued. 'He told me that on occasions through life I would meet with people who liked me, the chemistry would be good, the chat would flow, everything would be going fine. "Always remember David," said my father, "whenever that happens — never stay too long".' With that Kossof left the platform.

December 7

Among whom ye shine as lights in the world
PHILIPPIANS 2:15

It was a stormy night and a ship was coming into harbour at Cleveland in the United States. The lighthouse was shining brightly but the pilot on board could see that there were other lower lights, set on rocks around the shore, that were not shining.

'Where are the lower lights?' asked the captain anxiously.

'Gone out, sir,' replied the pilot.

'Can you make the harbour, then?' asked the captain.

'We must sir, or perish.'

. . . and perish many of them did. The lower lights were gone out and the ship was wrecked upon the rocks.

You, Christian, are a lower light. In your corner of life you are constantly warning the unconverted of dangers if they go on without the Lord Jesus. What if the lower lights are gone out?

169

December 8

And be not conformed to this world: but be ye transformed
. . .
ROMANS 12:2

Right through his word God clearly warns us not to live like the world around us. What does 'the world' mean? Certainly it does not mean planet earth. It does not mean we are to hate mountains, trees, rivers, meadows, woodland or the physical world around us. 'The world' referred to in the New Testament is the system of ideas and ways of living that are evil, against God and ruled by the devil and headed for hell. It is to copy the standards of lost people instead of living like the Lord Jesus. We are not to copy the fads and fashions of our selfish society.

'There is', said W. Pratney, 'no such thing as a worldly Christian.'

December 9

Let every man abide in the same calling wherein he was called
1 CORINTHIANS 7:20

Sometimes life can be monotonous. The housewife especially has to bid farewell to her husband every morning and turn to a stack of dishes, to dusting, mending, cooking, cleaning and ironing.

Many men have to do monotonous jobs, in industry especially, so monotonous in fact, that with due respect, a trained monkey could do the same job. Tens of thousands of young people have to go to school day after day: Mr. Brown for English, Mrs. Smith for French, Mr. Fraser for Maths, Mr. Arnold for Physics, Mrs. Moore for Chemistry.

Job monotony, or not, we serve the Lord Jesus Christ. So Christians do everything, heartily, as unto the Lord and know the joy of the Lord even in the midst of monotony!

As F. B. Meyer put it:

'If God opens the door to something else, of course use it. But if not, do not fret or chafe. Even if others pass thee, keep quiet and humble, and go on preparing thyself for thy great opportunity: and when it suddenly comes to thee, as it came to Joseph, thou wilt be prepared by thy behaviour in the prison to pass to the palace with its larger opportunities.'

December 10

Render therefore to all their dues
ROMANS 13:7

Today I want to pay tribute to my Headmaster at Down High School, Downpatrick which stands under the shadow of the old cathedral. Perhaps my tribute will encourage some 'weary' schoolteacher to know that their work is probably the most important in the world.

THE HEADMASTER

I remember that day very clearly. Our school was experiencing a wave of sadness which we had never known before. A boy in our class had been killed when riding his bicycle home from school on the 'Downpatrick Straight', as we called it. As decent a chap as you ever knew. It left us quite numb.

It so happened that we had the headmaster the period after assembly for geometry and we all wondered how he would ever teach. Teach! He taught us that morning an example of what it means when despite the tragedies of human life, we must go on. We must pick up the pieces and try again. It was his courage and control of things that so impressed us that day.

I was doing very badly at school. I was informed that as far as maths was concerned I was banging my head against a brick wall. Yet I desperately wanted to go to University. One day, taking up courage, I went down to his study and told him my desire. He smiled. 'If you are willing to work, I'll help you,' he said. So every week, after school, in the headmaster's study, I was drilled in the rudiments of geometry. He never deserted me until my exams were past.

As I recall my schooldays, my headmaster did not *need* to take any notice of me, but he did. He could have dismissed my childish dreams, but he didn't. He inspired them, encouraged them, and took time to help an insignificant being like me who could not possibly have been of any use to him.

I'm sure he often wondered if anybody ever really listened to his reading of the Scriptures at school assembly every day — thousands of us over the years remember listening very well. One of his favourite passages was from Ecclesiastes 3 'To everything there is a season . . . a time to be born, and a time to die; a time to weep, and a time to laugh.' From that famous passage I take a few words. There is 'a time to keep silent and a time to speak'. I would not have dared to write these things about my headmaster, Arthur Fowweather, a few years ago but there comes a time to speak, and gladly I have spoken.

December 11

Gather up the fragments that remain, that nothing be lost
JOHN 6:12

God never wastes his servant's pain.
God never wastes his servant's time.
God never wastes his servant's toil.
God never wastes his servant's gifts.

December 12

Inasmuch as ye have done it unto one of the least of these my brethren, ye have done it unto me
MATTHEW 25:40

He was some insignificant person. He was not one of the 'big names': he was not very talented, not a sparkling conversationalist. Uncouth, even. Yet for Jesus' sake and

172

for the fact that he was Christ's, you were kind to him. You laid aside your favourite journal and made him a cup of tea. You stopped your car on the way to that important function and gave him a lift into the city. You went out of your way to help. Has it ever occurred to you that you might as well have been doing deeds of kindness to the King of Kings as when you were doing them for one who may have been among the least of his brethren?

You seek, perhaps, some great thing to do for the Lord? Then turn today and do some little thing for the least of his brethren. They are one and the same thing.

December 13

Fear thou not; for I am with thee: be not dismayed; for I am thy God: I will strengthen thee; yea, I will help thee; yea, I will uphold thee with the right hand of my righteousness
ISAIAH 41:10

A friend rang me, recently. He had a very serious problem and had shared it with one whom he considered an undying friend. I knew the seriousness of his problem but I was shocked when he told me how his friend had reacted. He had been flippant, uncaring. His attitude to the problem could be summed up in the words — 'a gloss-over'. My friend was shattered.

God will never gloss-over your problem. No uncaring flippancy will cross his lips. Read today's text again. Such deep assurances and promises are far beyond the reaches of your local bank, your social security, your doctor, or even your 'undying friend'. He promises you in the midst of your problem, a clear head (no dismay), a transfusion of strength and protection against all the liars and deceivers who surround you. He will uphold you with the right hand of his righteousness.

173

December 14

But I keep under my body, and bring it into subjection
1 CORINTHIANS 9:27

To my fellow men — a heart of love.
To my God — a heart of flame.
To myself — a heart of steel.

Augustine

December 15

In season, out of season
2 TIMOTHY 4:2

Travelling around in Christian work I have come across a strange phenomenon. When arriving in some city or town and prior to commencing meetings I am often told — 'Unfortunately, this is a bad week for meetings. Monday night there is a huge football match on in town, Tuesday night there is a big pre-election rally, Wednesday night on TV there is the final episode of a popular Classic, Thursday is a general holiday in the area, on Friday the singing star Mr. X is at the local town hall and on Saturday, well, you know, Saturday nights!!' If I were to sit down with these people and discuss the matter, the first thing I would ask is: 'When was there ever a good week for meetings?'

They all start from the wrong point. The word of God, preached in the power of the Holy Spirit, is *always* suitable and adequate for the needs of human hearts in *any* week. We do not require to check the local paper or the TV Times to find out if it is suitable to preach his word. Others should be worried that there are Bible preaching meetings in town; not us! We should be a threat to them; not their attractions a threat to us.

174

December 16

Not with eyeservice, as menpleasers; but as servants of Christ, doing the will of God from the heart
EPHESIANS 6:6

They stoned Wesley when he preached Christ and yet, I have stood in a town where the Town Council have now raised a plaque to commemorate the fact! Led by *Punch*, the whole of the London press, week by week, tried to silence young Spurgeon, but that very same magazine laid a fine tribute on Spurgeon's grave.

Matthew Mead put it well when he wrote:

'If the preaching of Christ is to the world foolishness, then it is no wonder that the disciples of Christ are to the world fools. For according to the gospel, a man must die in order to live: he must be empty who would be full: he must be lost who would be found: he must have nothing who would have all things: he must be blind who would see: he must be condemned who would be redeemed. He is no true Christian who is not the world's fool.'

December 17

The same came to Jesus by night . . .
JOHN 3:2

We have been a bit hard on Nicodemus, have we not? We say he was scared, unprepared to commit himself to the Lord Jesus publicly so he came by night. Maybe we have judged him wrongly. Maybe he came to Jesus by night simply because he couldn't wait until the morning.

December 18

Read Psalm 22

In the Gospels we see the Cross of Christ from the point of view of the onlooker. In this psalm, prophetically, we enter

175

the mind and heart of Christ and discover just how he felt. It is an insight that draws deep gratitude for the sheer love of the Saviour for us. I have often drawn much blessing from Stevenson's outline of this psalm and in preaching it have been moved to see people seeking Christ afterwards. Stevenson has a sermon upon every verse.

1.	The Cry
2.	The Complaint
3.	The Acknowledgement
4-6.	The Contrast
6.	The Reproach
7.	The Mockery
8.	The Taunt
9 -10.	The Appeal
11.	The Entreaty
12 -13.	The Assault
14.	The Faintness
15.	The Exhaustion
16.	The Piercing
17.	The Emaciation
	The Insulting Gaze
18.	The Partition of the garments and casting lots
19-21.	The Importunity
21.	The Deliverance
22.	The Gratitude
23.	The Invitation
24.	The Testimony
25.	The Vow
26.	The Satisfaction of the Meek
	The Seekers of the Lord praising him
	The Eternal Life
27.	The Conversion of the world (not, note, Universal Salvation)
28.	The Enthronement
29.	The Author of the faith
30.	The Seed

31.   The Everlasting Theme
       and Occupation
       The Finisher of the faith

December 19

... and he was called the Friend of God
JAMES 2:23

        Forgive me, Lord
        When
        Fraternising with
        Fame, and
        Rubbing shoulders with
        Fellows who are famous
        Means more than this —
        The pinnacle of privilege
        Fellowship with the King of Kings
        And Lord of Lords —
        That heartfelt handclasp and
        'Inner circle' intimacy of
        Being deemed a
        Friend of God.

                            Alexandra Fay Hetherington
                                 (Lisburn, Co. Down)

December 20

Whose adorning ... let it be ... a meek and quiet spirit,
which is in the sight of God of great price
1 PETER 3:3, 4

    Beauty is a very handy thing to have,
    especially for a woman who isn't handsome.

December 21

The goodness of God leadeth thee to repentance
ROMANS 2:4

To do so, no more, is the truest repentance.

December 22

... to root out ...
JEREMIAH 1:10

Down near Lough Neagh, Ireland's most famous Lough, there lives a much respected Christian lady, Mrs. Patricia Emerson, known far and wide as 'Peggy'. Amongst a host of other responsibilities she attends to a large garden and has found that weeding has taught her many a spiritual lesson. I will let her tell you all about it just as she told it to me recently.

'I was weeding the garden when I discovered this lovely bright green leaf growing in abundance all over the place. "What's that nice plant?" I asked my husband who was giving me a hand. "That", said he, in a superior tone of voice, "is garden plague, and you won't think it's so nice when you have spent half the night trying to get it out." And do you know he was right.

'I started to pull and the lovely green leaves gave way to long white roots, that stretched and stretched and stretched, and by the time I had the bed of parsley weeded, the white roots completely hid the green leaves, and I couldn't help thinking how like this is to sin in our lives. How subtle it is, how pleasant it appears to be, how hard it is to get rid of and how very ugly it looks when it is eventually exposed.

'You know it's a funny thing, it's not the large weeds that are hard to remove. A good tug and you will get them out very successfully, but try to get out those small ones, and it's a different matter, and again I thought how like our lives. When we first come to know the Lord Jesus as our personal Saviour it's easy to give everything up for him. We are so anxious to please him that we surrender all our lives

178

to his service. But by and by the little weeds start, and they don't seem very important until suddenly we try to pull one out, and we discover that the nice little leaves are joined to long clinging roots, and we can't move them at all.

'So I decided wouldn't it be a good idea if we tried not to let the weeds grow in the first place? Let's try to keep the garden of our lives full of fragrance for him, let's make it a place where he can walk in the cool of the day, and we can show him every corner with not a weed in sight.'

December 23

Thou hast put gladness in my heart, more than in the time that their corn and their wine increased
PSALM 4:7

Some have too much, yet still do crave
I little have, and seek no more.
They are but poor though much they have,
And I am rich with little store.
They poor, I rich; they beg, I give;
They lack, I have; they pine, I live.

December 24

And Joseph also went up from Galilee, out of the city of Nazareth into Judea, unto the city of David . . . with Mary his espoused wife, being great with child
LUKE 2:4, 5

It is Christmas Eve. On this night across the world there are the sweet associations of holly and fir, the memory of deep woods, of peaceful hills and of mantling snow. The air is full of expectancy, the stars have a deeper meaning as they twinkle through the living-room window. The children are beside themselves. It is the Eve of Christmas.

I once stood on the Judean hillside and looked up to Bethlehem on the hill. The mystery of the incarnation, the story of the birth of the Saviour was as precious to me on that hot summer afternoon in Israel as it is when I read about it to my family by my own fireside on Christmas Eve. The barrenness of the Judean wilderness around did not sour the sweetness of that mystery of mysteries: God manifest in flesh. It made its reality all the more real.

The hinge of history was on the door of that Bethlehem stable, the simple shepherds heard the voice of an angel and found their Lamb: the wise men saw the light of a star and found their Wisdom. The fact of Jesus' coming is the final and unanswerable proof that God cares but let us remember that Christmas is not just about the birth of a baby; it is the heavenly Father saying goodbye to his Son. Christmas is a Son away from home: away from home to die. The shadow of Calvary looms over that Judean hillside.

December 25

He shall be great, and shall be called the Son of the Highest
LUKE 1:32

Nothing could have been more humble. A Jewish child wound up in bandages and lying in a trough where oxen feed. It was, no doubt, a smelly place. Not much of a place to talk of greatness, is it?

I mean, take King Herod who lived at that time. Many people thought he was great. He gloried his name everywhere with harbours and fortresses, amphitheatres, gymnasiums, statues and monuments. He had a stately home with gold, jewels and white marble and all that. Herod the Great he was called.

Think a minute. Where are his harbours, fortresses and amphitheatres now? They have all crumbled to dust and any bricks that are left have become mere Mediterranean rubble.

And what of the Jewish child? What did he do with his life? He gave his life as ransom for many. During his earthly life he went about helping little children, healing sick folk and doing good. In him was no sin. Through his death at Calvary millions have found peace and forgiveness of sins and have received eternal life.

What, during this Christmas Day, will you do then with Jesus which is called Christ? A Christless Christmas is bad enough, but a Christless Eternity is the ultimate tragedy.

Receive him as Saviour today. Come let us adore him!

December 26

Yea, let him take all, forasmuch as my lord the king is come again in peace unto his own house
2 SAMUEL 19:30

Today your mind starts turning towards the New Year. What will your personal future hold?

On this Boxing Day I turn your eyes and heart to what may seem a very ordinary little verse. Tucked away in the life of David it concerns Mephibosheth the injured son of Jonathan. Not only was Mephibosheth injured on both his feet but the man appointed by David to look after him had injured his reputation as well: he lied about him. He had told David that Mephibosheth had been disloyal to him and David believed the lie.

When David found out the truth he immediately offered Mephibosheth material reward: he would have the land he had lost through the lies told against him. It is the answer which Mephibosheth gave which concerns me today. Mephibosheth turned round to David and said 'I don't care one little bit about land, David, all I care about is you. I'm quite content now, David, just as long as you are on the throne. Let that liar have all the land he wants, it's not land I'm interested in.'

If Christians lived with such an attitude it would be better for them! Surely all we should be concerned about is that *our* King, the Lord Jesus, should have rightful place on the throne of our lives. What do we care if liars all around connive or lie and cheat in order to gain material reward? If

181

that is what they're after, let them. You and I have a greater purpose: that in all things he may have the pre-eminence. This is our aim and with this at the centre of our lives, things at the circumference will be in their right priority and take care of themselves, even material things.

December 27

When they shall be hungry, they shall fret
ISAIAH 8:21

There once was a Christian here in Ulster who was very adamant about what he would eat and what he wouldn't eat. He even argued in the presence of a friend of mine about the matter and bandied Scriptures about in his talk. My wise friend was asked about what he would eat or refuse.

'That would all depend on just how hungry I was,' he answered, quietly.

Indeed it would. Hunger finds no fault in the cooking and finds raw beans a relish. Remember that while you may have plenty, millions upon millions of people across the world, this very day, starve.

December 28

Doth not he see my ways, and count all my steps? If I have walked with vanity, or if my foot hath hasted to deceit . . .?
JOB 31:4, 5

The steps of a good man are ordered by the Lord
PSALM 37:23

Did Titus make a gain of you? . . . walked we not in the same steps?

2 CORINTHIANS 12:18

Christ also suffered for us, leaving us an example, that we should follow his steps

1 PETER 2:21

December 29

Like as a father pitieth his children, so the Lord pitieth them that fear him
PSALM 103:13

I must say that one of the hardest things I find I have to do at this time in my life is to leave my small children to go out at night. I am heartened to know that other fathers feel the same way, because Dr Barnhouse tells of going out one evening, leaving his children in the care of a baby-sitter. When he returned about midnight the girl was greatly concerned that the Barnhouses' eldest child had been crying for about four hours. Dr Barnhouse went to the child's room and found her flushed and sobbing, her face red with long weeping. When her father picked her up she threw her arms around his neck and sobbed: 'Daddy, say it isn't true. You do love me.' He replied that of course he loved her, and the child then continued, 'She said that if I was bad you wouldn't love me, and I know that I've been bad, so maybe you do not love me.'

Dr Barnhouse pressed his child to him and said, 'My dear child, I always love you. When you are good I love you with a love that makes me glad; when you are bad I love you with a love that makes me sad. But I love you, good or bad.' The child quietly calmed down, a smile came and she was soon fast asleep.

December 30

As though God did beseech you by us: we pray you in Christ's stead, be ye reconciled to God
2 CORINTHIANS 5:20

We do not stand in the world bearing witness to Christ: we stand in Christ bearing witness to the world.

Ralph L. Williams

December 31

Even so, come, Lord Jesus
REVELATION 22:20

We began this year together, you and I, and now we must part. When writing this book I have often wondered just what you look like. You may be a new Christian or you may have known the Lord for many a long day. I do not know. I only pray that something said in this book has touched your life, some thought shared has got down into your heart and drawn you closer to the Saviour.

Perhaps you live far away from the mountains where I live, far away in some city, town or village seeking to honour, in all your ways, the One who died for you. God bless you, encourage you and inspire you to go on for him. Nothing else counts eternally, only what's done for the Lord Jesus will last.

I pray that in the coming days you and I will live in such a way that our eyes will be often looking towards the horizon, waiting and looking for our soon coming Lord. I pray we will not shrink from him in shame but rise up joyfully to greet him.

Meantime his mercies will continue, new every morning, sure as the sunrise, until his day dawns and then, I am assured, we will know no more sunrise for in that eternal land they have no need of the sun, the Lamb is the light thereof. Even so, come, Lord Jesus. Perhaps today!